THE SPIRITUAL LIFE

STUDIES IN THE
SCIENCE OF RELIGION

By GEORGE A. COE, Ph.D.

John Evans Professor of Moral and Intellectual Philosophy
in Northwestern University

New York: Eaton & Mains
Cincinnati: Jennings & Pye
1900

Copyright by
EATON & MAINS,
1900.

EATON & MAINS PRESS,
150 Fifth Avenue, New York.

PREFACE

THE studies here presented have been undertaken in response to a conviction that, in the interest of both science and religion, a new intellectual attitude is necessary with respect to the facts of the spiritual life. The religious processes taking place around us and within us must be observed with all the precision that modern psychological methods and tools render possible. For, whatever else religion may or may not be, it is at least a mass of ascertainable states of consciousness; and in the absence of information to the contrary we must presume that such states can be analyzed and described, and that their relations to one another and to the recognized laws of the mental and bodily life can be to some extent determined. What is needed is an examination of the facts as such, without reference to their possible bearing upon theology or philosophy. Until this work is done there will remain an important gap in the scientific knowledge of man. For, clearly, it is the humanity that now is that gives us our problems concerning man's origin and development, and that necessarily controls and tests our hypotheses. Similarly, knowledge of what religion now is must be the most illuminating factor in any satisfactory science of religion.

Religious propagandism also has a decisive motive for seeking to understand the religious consciousness of to-day. Ignorance is sometimes power, it is true, but, on the whole, the safer course in a good cause is to trust in knowledge. Moreover, aside from this general motive there is special need for the kind of knowledge here in question. Current events are forcing upon thoughtful minds in all the Protestant Churches a suspicion, if not a conviction, that what has claimed a peculiar right to the name "evangelical," both in piety and in modes of propagating the Gospel, has not fully solved its own chosen problems. There is reason for doubting whether even the spiritual teachers and guides of the people really grasp the mental processes with which they have to deal. Training in doctrine, in philosophy, in history, and even in the questions of the day, constitutes only a logical equipment; there is still necessary a psychological equipment in order that one may appreciate the vast mass of mental states and processes of a nonlogical sort. The evident decay of the revival, the alienation from the Church of whole classes of the population, the excess of women over men in Church life, the apparent powerlessness of organized religion to suppress or seriously check the great organized vices and injustices of society, the failure of the Sunday school to make the people or even its own pupils familiar with the contents of the Bible—these facts ought to raise a question as to what, among the matters upon which we have laid stress, is really practical and what mere ignorant blundering.

This question is already being raised, and it is bound to be asked more and more often and in louder and louder tones. It is no sign of enmity toward the Church or of coldness toward Christianity, but rather an incident of the expanding spirituality of men who find in Jesus the final meaning of life, and in evangelical Christianity the essential germ of future religious progress. This germ demands to be understood. It is necessary to perceive that the problems here suggested do not concern matters of mere temporary expediency. They go to the bottom of life; they concern the very essence of religion, of religious forces, and of the mind in which religion lives and through which it works for the healing of the nations. If this be true there is not a ray of reasonable hope for the solution of these problems unless in some way—either by a happy hit of uninstructed zeal or else by definite knowledge of the psychical factors involved—we manage to put ourselves into line with the mind of man as it is.

The present volume does not undertake to solve these problems, much less to present a systematic or complete treatment of the general psychology of religion. My task has been the much less ambitious one of working out a few closely related groups of facts which will claim a place in the systematic psychology of religion when this comes to be written, and which in the meantime have an important bearing upon the practical side of religious life and work. While I have tried to approach the facts in the spirit and by the methods of science, I have not hesitated to point out in each chapter some of the practical uses to which its materials and results may be put. I hope that these suggestions will show where to look for a practical solution of several of our most troublesome problems.

I am under obligation to the editors of *The Psychological Review* for permission to reprint in Chapter III, with alterations and additions, an article that was published in the September, 1899, number of that journal.

GEORGE A. COE.

Evanston, Illinois.

8

CONTENTS

CONTENTS

INTRODUCTION

The Psychological Point of View

PERHAPS no group of ascertained facts excels in either theoretical or practical interest the mass of human experiences called religious. Clustering about them and intertwined with them are all the marvels, real and alleged, of hypnotism, telepathy, and mediumship; illusions and hallucinations here acquire their greatest power; here the roots of the highest reason lie side by side with those of the lowest superstition. Nor do religious phenomena lose their psychological importance when they are disentangled from everything that is abnormal, for they are everywhere present in human life, and in forms exceedingly various. In some of these forms religious experiences are rare, sudden, and surprising; in all forms they reverberate with surprising power and permanence through the entire mental organism.

Yet the phenomena of religious experience have been the last to be granted a hearing by the science of psychology. Explorations have been carried on in many a remote and obscure region of the mind in apparent unconsciousness of this whole mass of psychical wonders lying at the door of the psychologist's study. Metaphysics speculated about the rational basis of religion; the philosophy of religion mingled these speculations with some slight analysis of the states of mind called religious; theology appealed, in a general way, to religious experience in verification of its theories; the history and science of religion rummaged museums of anthropology and dug about the roots of language in order to discover the earliest forms of religion: but to none of these was it revealed that the surest way to understand religion is to observe its present manifestations. What was still needed was the

Application of Empirical Methods to Present Religious Phenomena.

Revival preachers took the first step in this method when they gathered statistics concerning the age at which large numbers of persons were converted. It is probable that this incipient application of scientific method was more effective in awakening sinners than any equal amount of labor expended upon theorizing or arguing in the absence of systematic observation of facts.

The first comprehensive and organized impulse to a scientific study of the religious phenomena in the midst of which we are living made its appearance in the present decade. In 1891 President G. Stanley Hall, of Clark University, published an article on the moral and religious training of children[1] based directly upon the psychology of childhood and adolescence. Several pupils of his followed with further observations and analyses.[2] Especially worthy of mention for the range and patient impartiality of his work is E. D. Starbuck,[3] now of Stanford University. It would be easy to over or under estimate the value of the results thus attained, but this at least may be claimed: We have here the crude beginnings of an empirical psychology of religious experience.

The method employed by these workers is, first, to secure from hundreds of persons a written description of such facts as their conversion, their religious growth, their conception of God, their doubts, etc. These descriptions are then analyzed, and the results are grouped and massed in various ways so as to exhibit averages and tendencies in religious life. Somewhat secure results have thus been attained, with regard to the probability of conversion at various ages, and suggestive material concerning motives, feelings, doubts, and the effects of various influences.

---

[1] *Pedagogical Seminary*, i, 196ff.

[2] A. H. Daniels, " The New Life," in *American Journal of Psychology*, 1893, vi, 61ff.; J. H. Leuba, " A Study in the Psychology of Religious Phenomena," *ibid.*, 1896, vii, 309ff. See, also, Luther Gulick, " Age, Sex, and Conversion," in *Association Outlook* for December, 1897; W. H. Burnham, " The Study of Adolescence," in *Pedagogical Seminary*, i, 2 ; E. G. Lancaster, "Psychology and Pedagogy of Adolescence," in *Pedagogical Seminary*, v, 1.

[3] " A Study of Conversion," in *American Journal of Psychology*, 1897, viii, 268ff.; " Some Aspects of Religious Growth," *ibid.*, ix, 70ff.; *The Psychology of Religion*, London, 1899, pp. xx, 423. This last contribution to the psychology of religion appears as these studies are passing through the press. I regret that I cannot give it fuller notice.

This is called the *questionnaire* method. That it is an effective way of getting at some kinds of facts is evident, but its capacity as a tool for investigation is obviously limited to such facts as the writers of the papers are competent to observe and describe with scientific accuracy. The average person of intelligence is qualified, of course, to testify regarding the more external facts of his religious experience, such as dates, persons, and circumstances, but in the absence of specific training in self-observation few persons are qualified to give even approximately correct information regarding the subjective processes that constitute their religious experience. To explain why this is so would necessitate a larger excursion into general psychology than is possible in this place. It must suffice to say that in one's own mind, just as in nature, the finer differences, so important when accuracy is in question, escape attention unless the observer has been trained to look for them; that various processes of self-laudation, of self-excusing, of self-condemning, of explanation, of accommodation to the opinions of others or of revolt from such opinions—all these so mingle with the facts as to blur, suppress, magnify, and distort what is actually going on within; that, finally, memory has many peculiar and very effective ways of falsely representing the past. On all these accounts it is necessary, when the inner history is in question, to secure some corrective for the self-deceptions that may easily creep into the narrative of the most honest and, in other matters, most competent witness. The present studies will illustrate how some other methods of investigation can be combined with that which rests upon question and answer.

Whatever the method of securing and analyzing the data may be, there can be no reasonable doubt of the necessity of going for information directly to the facts that can be observed here and now. No appeal to the Bible can answer our questions unless the Bible is a book of science, or at least of scientific observations. Happily for the peace and progress of investigations in the sphere of religion, we are coming to understand that the Scriptures are given for instruction in righteousness, not for instruction in any science, even psychology and the science of religion. Data for all the sciences of man we certainly find there, but not scientific doctrines, nor, indeed, the scientific purpose and attitude. The Bible is a bank rather than a theory of finance; it is religion rather than a theory of religion. The way is open, then, and the time has arrived for applying to the phenomena of the religious life the approved methods of the empirical sciences.

Psychology and the Supernatural.

The proposal to apply scientific methods to the study of the most sacred experiences of life may possibly raise the question whether conversion and other religious phenomena are not thereby assumed to be purely natural occurrences in which God has no direct part. Reduced to its lowest terms, the problem is whether the empirical method of getting at facts implies that such facts are not due to divine influences.

As a general reply it might be sufficient to point out that, even in the investigation of physical facts, the sciences assume nothing whatever as to the presence or absence of God in nature. If we may assume that winds and tides, and day and night, do not occur hit-or-miss, but only under specific circumstances— if we may assume that the world is a cosmos and not a chaos—we may be indifferent, as scientific men, as to whether the phenomena of nature are due to divine power or not. What science looks for is law, in the sense of uniformities among phenomena. Now, to look for possible uniformities among religious phenomena is not to make any assumption as to the real agents involved. It is simply to assume that religious experiences are not a chaotic mass in which consequents have no respect for antecedents.

Looking a bit deeper into the problem, we may ask whether a denial of this one assumption would not be essentially atheistic. What a strange inversion of faith is that which looks for the Infinite Mind in chaos rather than in cosmos! Surely God, as a rational being, will be self-consistent, will act in the

16

same way under the same circumstances. If, then, there were no uniformities in religious experience, the inference would be that religion itself proceeded from some disorderly or mischievous spirit rather than from the Father of Lights, with whom is no variableness. It may be worth while, also, to remind ourselves now and then that facts are facts, and that no amount of theorizing about how they must be can prevent or refute observation of how they actually are. The "armed eye" of science no man can close, and he who attempts to do so should reflect upon how he thereby discredits his own beliefs.

Empirical methods do not, then, reduce the facts of the religious life to the plane of the natural as contrasted with the supernatural. Every question arising in the psychology of religious experience may be understood in this way: Under what circumstances does the Divine Spirit work such or such a change in the minds of men? That the Holy Spirit does observe antecedents and wait for conditions to ripen; that he does not vouchsafe the same blessings to all individuals or to all ages of life; and that we have it in our power either to prepare the way for his revelations or to hinder them—all this is current belief among Christians. Now, these are the very uniformities that need investigating. In fact, psychology can only render more precise and complete what is already recognized in a partial way in the practice of the religious life. Yet the results will not be doc-

trinal in the ordinary sense of the term. They will
be merely statements of uniformities existing between certain antecedents and certain consequents,
and will leave entirely open the vast field of questions
regarding the divine purposes toward men and regarding man's real nature and destiny.

Religious Psychology as Equipment for Religious Work.

The importance of such knowledge for one who
has the care of souls is evident. At the point where
the theologian becomes a winner and guide of men,
there definite knowledge of men turns into current
coin. Every item of information concerning any
uniformity existing between a certain experience
and its conditions becomes a lever for controlling
the experience itself.

In his efforts to adapt himself to the variegated
needs of men the religious worker has heretofore
been obliged to rely almost entirely upon instinctive
sympathy with human nature and the tact that sometimes blossoms out of it. Generally the worker
makes his own experience a standard by which to
judge and to guide the experience of others—as
though the many members of Christ's body, in spite
of their diversity of gifts and of duties, must nevertheless have the same form of experience. In one
case falling under my knowledge this form of inference was employed in a novel way. A young man,

who on three different occasions had earnestly sought
to be converted and had failed to receive what his
advisers told him to expect, reasoned as follows: "I
have honestly met all the conditions laid down, but
have not experienced what I have been taught to
look for. I am not different from other men. Therefore, since I have not received the blessing, neither
have they. The whole thing is a mistake or a sham!"
Both he and his spiritual guides had committed the
fallacy of reasoning from insufficient data. And it
is not easy to see how the evil effects of this error can
be eliminated from religious work unless at least the
leaders of such work take the trouble to study the religious mind in a broadly inductive manner.

So far as I am informed, practically the only definite and communicable scheme of adaptation to personal needs now in use consists in marshaling regi-
ments of Scripture texts with which to fight all kinds
of doubt, hesitation, and objection. Whatever virtues this practice may possess, it certainly suffers
from one serious defect, that it studies texts rather
than human nature. It does not ask *whence* the
doubt, hesitation, or objection; it does not seek the
conditions in order to remove or alleviate *them,* but
fires directly at the results. If a homely simile may
be pardoned, our ordinary revival methods may be
compared with the packages of proprietary medicines to be found on the shelves of any drug store.
Glance along the shelf and you will find the symp-

toms of almost any common disease described with apparent accuracy; and for each difficulty here is a specific, neatly wrapped up, provided with directions for taking, and in many cases with a corkscrew for unlocking the riches within. It need not be doubted that multitudes of persons have been really helped by doses from such bottles. The vice of this style of medication lies in the fact of the entire absence of competent diagnosis, of competent knowledge of the properties of the remedy, and of reasonable certainty that the remedy fits the patient. Similarly, many a revival worker is equipped with texts and advice and exhortation, all neatly classified and ready for application; but the investigation of the cases is utterly superficial, and no connection is ordinarily established between the remedy and the difficulty. Of course, some will say that the method approves itself by its results. But the same may be said for "patent" medicines. After all, the question is not merely whether we get results, but rather whether we get the best results and the most of them. For this, knowledge is necessary in the "cure of souls" as in the healing of bodies. How, then, should we excuse ourselves if, in order to bodily health, we should study anatomy and physiology with diligence while neglecting to know that more delicate organism, the mind, which is the seat of our spiritual weal or woe?

It is well to remember, too, that in both spheres the

negative cases are as significant as the positive ones.
We must ask not only how many persons we reach
by the revival, but also how many we fail to reach;
and we must hold ourselves to a rigid accountability
for the souls whom our defective methods get into
doubt and difficulty, or even repel from religion altogether. At a subsequent point in our discussion we
shall see that this question of the negative results of
well-meant efforts is by no means fanciful or gratui-
tous. So far, in fact, are these maladjustments from
being merely occasional or rare that the question will
at last press itself upon us whether certain widely
approved customs do not quite as often beget throes
of disappointment and unrest as the peace and confidence of the sons of God.

Why should not the care of souls become an art—
a system of organized and proportioned methods
based upon definite knowledge of the material to be
wrought upon, the ends to be attained, and the means
and instruments for attaining them? Such an art
would require scientific insight into the general organization of the mind, and especially into the particular characteristics of the child mind, the youth
mind, and the mature mind. It would know how to
discriminate between normal and morbid states of
religious feeling, would understand the intimate in-
terrelations between the spiritual and the physical
life, would observe the temperamental and other differences between individuals, and would appreciate

the difference between symmetrical development of all the faculties and the various kinds of spiritual one-sidedness. The religious artist will study when and how and how far to administer instruction to the intellect, incitement to the feelings, and stimulus to the will. The workman who needeth not to be ashamed must know how rightly to divide. Of course, he must also have an experience of his own, intimacy with the Scriptures, and inspiration. Neither knowledge without zeal nor zeal without knowledge will suffice. But, given the scientific knowledge for which a plea is here uttered, together with these other qualifications, and mixed with a reasonable amount of sympathy and tact, we have the artist as distinguished from the mere mechanic.

Now, this knowledge which undergirds the art of religious culture cannot all be derived from speculative philosophy or from any of the traditional branches of theological instruction. Philosophy and theology do, indeed, have many important things to tell the religious worker. Not seldom, through ignorance of the history of philosophic and theologic thought, religious instruction becomes little less than farcical; but fully as often it goes astray from ignorance of the workings of the human mind. On the other hand, here and there can be found a leader whose finer tact or intuition has enabled him to acquire much of the necessary insight from hand-to-hand contact with the problems and difficulties of his calling. This, however, is a laborious way of learning, and meantime, though one use one's own errors as stepping-stones to better things, the errors themselves can never be quite nullified. Everything, in short, goes to show how great is the practical need of a psychology of the religious life.

The Psychology of Religion as a Clew to Existing Religious Unrest.

It is an ancient habit of religionists to try to understand everything by its relation to the accepted standards of belief. Give any new or old movement its correct theological classification and it is supposed to be thereby adequately construed. Accordingly, the weapons which the average religious teacher almost always employs against supposedly erroneous systems are dialectic darts. The best current example is the treatment just now being accorded to Christian Science by the orthodox clergy. The clergy apparently believe that, if only the so-called philosophy underlying Christian Science can be proved to be absurd, the inroads of this new sect can be stopped. But neither the results in this case nor human experience in general indicate the wisdom or adequacy of this style of attack. It would be a very great delusion to suppose that such movements make progress chiefly by convincing the rational intellect, or that they can be stopped by a counter appeal of the same sort. The human being to whom religions appeal is not

23

merely, or chiefly, intellect, but rather a highly complex organism of feelings and affections, impulses and aspirations, habits and instincts. The theology, or intellectual part, of a religion is sure to have some connection with these other factors of real life, but it is not the engine that keeps them going; rather, they are the engine that keeps it going. To speak more accurately, the intellectual and other factors exist together in a complex, each having some determining part in the total outcome, but the purely intellectual factor is less influential than the others. It is the explanation rather than the thing to be explained; the weapon rather than the thing to be defended.

What has just been said of Christian Science is true also of most, perhaps all, of the supposedly aberrant cults and substitutes for cults of which our day is so prolific. Spiritualism, theosophy, the religion of positivism, the ethical society movement, faith cure, and all the others touch the human soul at many points. In other words, they can be understood and practically dealt with only by studying them from the psychological standpoint. We have already learned that the proper question with regard to such movements is never "Is it true, or false?" for we know that large groups of men are never captivated for any length of time by absolute error. Every system of belief is partly true and partly false. But the time has now come when we ought to grasp a still

24

larger truth, widen out our horizon still further. We must somehow come to *feel* with those from whom we differ however profoundly; we must somehow trace out their processes of mental manufacture— noting how the power is carried from wheel to band, from band to shaft, from shaft and band to this machine and that, each of which contributes something to the finished product. Truly this is a far more delicate and complicated and pains-demanding task than the mere logical anatomizing of a system of beliefs; but its outcome is correspondingly richer. It brings us closer to life in its concreteness; it opens avenues of sympathy, and, should heaven give us the mission of correcting error, it shows us how to reach the total cause and not merely one or two of its symptoms.

Furthermore, we sadly need to understand the great mass of persons who have cut loose from all forms of organized religion. Experience seems to show that we cannot hope to win them back by either wailing or scolding or arguing or coddling. We must now begin at the other end—find out what we have to deal with before we hasten to adopt expedients. What is the state of mind of these persons? Is the religious instinct lacking in them? Are they deliberately stifling their highest aspirations? How do they feel when they think of God, of death, of the facts of life? Have they found some substitute for the Church which seems to yield the satis-

faction which the religious instinct craves? What
do they teach their children, and what do they desire their children to be like? Here, once more,
nothing short of the psychological standpoint gives
any promise of the needed insight and the needed
leverage.

Finally, we need to understand our own Church
life better than we do. Much that characterizes the
Churches has its origin, of course, in their respective
creeds, and must be understood from the doctrinal
standpoint; but much more has its origin elsewhere.
The soul strives always to utter its whole self, and
when perfect religion is attained it will be found to
be the center and unity and life energy of whatever
is worthy to be called human. Which side or sides
of this spherical religious instinct are most cultivated
in each of the denominations? How far do we en-
courage the life of contemplation? how far the life
of action? What states of mind are expressed in our
favorite songs? What are our ethical ideals? What
classes of society come to church; what services do
they attend, and why? In what proportion do the
two sexes participate in the various forms of activity
and life? These questions could easily be multiplied
to a hundred, every one of which would name an important practical problem that requires psychological
analysis for its answering.

This sketch of some of the possible services of
a psychology of the religious life is not the proc-

lamation of a program of any kind. As far as the present studies are concerned, it merely indicates some of the practical aspirations that have controlled the selection of a few topics out of the whole vast field.

27

THE SPIRITUAL LIFE

CHAPTER I

A Study of Religious Awakening

THE most striking of the definitely established results reached by the group of pioneer investigators mentioned in the Introduction is that there exists a general coordination between personal religious development and the chief periods of physical and mental growth. Whoever stops to reflect upon the commonest facts of childhood must perceive that, in the nature of things, childhood religion must differ from the religion of adult life. But this most general observation is insufficient to furnish a basis for settling the various questions connected with religious training. For this purpose it is essential that we define the epochs of growth, recognize the marks of transition, and determine the special characteristics tendencies and difficulties of each period.

Thus much the merest common sense would seem to dictate. Nevertheless, even in these days one sometimes meets with religious teaching that calls for practically the same type of religious experience in persons of all ages. It is even regarded as a fine thing when a child of seven or ten passes through paroxysms of repentance and conversion and afterward talks and prays like a grown person. I say this not from hearsay, but from my own observation. When, in addition, such a child assumes the airs of a preacher, and exhorts men to flee from the wrath to come—as recently happened, it is said, with a child of five years in the city of Chicago—the satisfaction of some misguided parents and teachers knows no bounds. For the most part, this particular kind of foolishness has died a natural death; yet who shall say that parents and teachers yet know what they ought to look for in childhood religion? There is, in fact, a widespread desire to know what children should be taught about God and salvation, what religious exercises should be required of them, and how far their impulses of various kinds should be trusted and how far restrained. Nothing short of a treatise would answer all such questions; yet the fundamental truth that should be controlling can be stated in a few words. The whole question goes back, finally, to the psychologist. Tell me wherein the child mind differs from the mind of youth and of adult, and, particularly, tell me how the child mind unfolds into the youth mind, and the rest will be a matter of inference joined with the ever-necessary inventiveness and tact.

"When I was a child, . . . I thought as a child."

To begin with, we may roughly divide the period
of about twenty-four years that elapses before full
maturity is attained into two subperiods of twelve
years each: the period of childhood and that of
youth, or adolescence. To assume, as is commonly
done, that the difference between these two is chiefly
physiological is a complete mistake; for along with
the physiological characteristics of each period go
mental traits equally well marked. The transition,
moreover, from childhood to youth is as profound
an affair mentally as it is physically. Let us note
briefly how the mental and the physical are correlated.

The child, considered as a member of an animal
species, is incapable of social functions. He is re-
stricted to physical individualism. He is not yet a
whole human being, but is rather, to adopt the words
of another, "a candidate for humanity." His mental
functions are correspondingly limited. He is dependent in mind as he is in body. As his elders provide his food, so they provide his ideas. He is a
creature of impressions rather than of reasons; although his exuberant activity may express itself in
the form of apparently profound questions, these are
rarely of vital concern. Few healthy children will
lose sleep because they cannot solve such problems.

Similarly, his moral life is largely dependent and
individualistic. This is, therefore, the time for pre-

cepts and the formation of habits of obedience. His attention is taken up with particular things to be done or to be avoided. It has not occurred to him to ask for the meaning of life as a whole, or to question the authority that is customary. He looks without and not within; at the near rather than the remote; at the present rather than the future. In a word, he does not realize, either in thought, feeling, or conduct, the organic relation of the human individual to the race, to nature, and to God.

Childhood religion is normally such as can fit into such a mind without strain or distortion. The child is able to take God for granted just because God is mentioned to him; but, to the child, God is a particular being among other beings, even one to be teased, cajoled, or deceived. When a storm-cloud threatens to break up a game there is prayer to avert the rain. Of course, childhood is not mistaken in thus thinking of the All-Father; it merely conceives him by means of childish faculties and gives him a natural and proper place within a child's stock of ideas. I have questioned many persons as to whether in their childhood God seemed to speak through their consciences, but in very few cases have I received affirmative answers. In general, also, the child "says" its prayers, not being able so much as to guess what prayer is to one who knows the stress and strain of life. Religious duties are gone through with much as the calisthenic or singing exercises at school. Depth of personal interest, of personal understanding, or of personal decision is not likely to be there unless growth is forced by unnatural instruction or by some unnatural burden upon the nervous system.

At about the age of twelve, though frequently before it, especially in the case of girls, strange premonitions begin to be felt. The child can no longer be completely naïve, individualistic, or unconscious of himself. He can no longer take the world and himself for granted. This is a prophecy of a momentous experience. During the next three or four years there is to come a transformation of the mental as well as of the physical organism more profound than any other between birth and death. New kinds of sensation and of emotion, new modes of thought, new attitudes of will, new meanings in life, new problems of duty, new kinds of temptation, new mysteries in religion—all these to come in a flood over the young adolescent. Some one has said of mental adolescence that it is as if we were born over again, not from an unremembered past into which the new life can bring no surprises, but from one conscious life into another that cannot be understood by anything in our previous experience.

In many ways this is undoubtedly the most critical period in the whole development of the individual. We should therefore expect to find the training of the child, especially as he approaches puberty, organized and guided so as to prepare him for this singular experience. To lessen the shock of the sexual awakening, and to prepare beforehand for its new temptations, we should expect parents to impart, long before such knowledge can become an irritant, the essential facts regarding the nature of sex. In a subsequent study I shall show how direct is the bearing of this point upon religious development during youth. There can be few greater unkindnesses to a youth than to permit him to meet and to deal with the profoundest fact of his physical being without ever having received from a pure and authoritative source a single item of information regarding it. On the part of parents and teachers unusual sympathy is demanded during these trying transition years. We should expect all the guides of the child to understand him, and to let him know that he is understood, so that he may freely ask advice. We should expect to find his school tasks and other tasks, his plays, his home life, his church life, and his social life all arranged and supervised with special reference to his stage of growth. To ask whether the church, the school, or the home satisfies these reasonable expectations is less the putting of a question than the proclamation of an indictment. We have not so much as taken the trouble to understand the period of youth; how, then, can we expect to conserve and promote its moral and religious values? What is first of all needful is to understand the—

Mental Characteristics of Adolescence.

The term adolescence, as now commonly used by psychologists, designates the whole period of approximately a dozen years from the first premonitions of puberty to the completion of the change to adult life.[1] The mental development during this period is directly correlated with the physical. As the child now comes into possession of all the powers that belong to the species, and thus becomes a determining factor in it, so his feelings and his intellectual horizon rapidly widen out. There is greater independence, and yet greater consciousness of social dependence. The social instinct, in fact, now for the first time comes to blossom. There enters into the life a new sense of how others think and feel, and a self-conscious effort after social life and social adjustment. Life means more. Naïvely individualistic the youth cannot be; if he is selfish, it is only by a more or less conscious wrenching of himself out of his normal adjustment.

We found the child mind occupied with impressions, and caring little for the universal. It is just the other way with the mind of the youth. The universal infatuates him, while the particular is likely to appear as a delay and a hindrance. He becomes a dreamer enamored of ideals and ravished with ambitions. Nothing but the greatest is great enough

---

[1] On this use of the term, see W. H. Burnham, in *Pedagogical Seminary*, i, 174ff., and E. G. Lancaster, *ibid.*, vi, 6iff.

for him; nothing but the perfect has any worth or beauty. When he was a child his attention was absorbed by the things about him; but now the new feelings and powers blossoming within him direct his mind inward, and he becomes self-conscious, bashful, introspective, critical. The most prominent thing about him is sensibility, and this may become so acute that he shrinks from life, conceals himself, and eats his own heart in solitude. He may become incommunicative, secretive, lonely, or he may seek support in the friendship of a clique of youths who, being of his own age, can appreciate him.

Just as the youth's own life grows inward, the things about him get an inner side also. It is now that beauty in nature assumes its mystical, fascinating quality. He thinks of things as having mysterious ultimate principles which he would fain penetrate. He has confidence in his ability to understand all mysteries if only he could get the right clew. He no longer takes things merely as they appear, nor is he willing to take anything for granted. Nothing short of absolute, indubitable truth, the true inwardness, the complete subjectivizing of everything, can satisfy him. Nothing short of absolutely right conduct can be right at all. He hates all imperfections, all compromises. What other persons call prudence seems to him to be disloyalty to principle. He will penetrate to the heart of moral law. Heretofore morality has imposed itself from outside, and right

36

conduct has consisted in obedience to formal rules; but now he begins to inspect the rules themselves, and, though he may question them, he finds within his own breast a lawgiver more exacting and terrible than any external rules. Though he passes out from under the tutelage of social law, he approaches in his own consciousness only so much nearer the awful seat of right.

It is now that he becomes a conscious logician. A passion for argumentation takes possession of him. He will settle everything by rigorous logic. It was at this period of life that Descartes entered upon the course of thought that produced his principle of doubting everything that can be doubted. The adolescent is a remorseless critic. There is no limit to his captiousness and censoriousness. The least slip in pronunciation, the least infelicity of rhetoric, the least fault in dress, in manners, or in conduct, is seized upon wherever found, and playmates, teachers, pastor, and parents pass under the rod of his scorn. Then appear pride, conceit, self-will, and rebellion against authority.

But all this time the youngster has been applying this whole merciless process to himself. He debates with himself more than with anyone else. He criticises himself; he agonizes for his faults. Most of all, perhaps, he will wring the secret of existence from himself. The childish "why," which used to be asked out of playful curiosity, has now given place to a serious questioning upon which the issues of life and of death appear to hang. And because the "why" of life does not respond to his insistent pleadings he becomes puzzled and perplexed, possibly impatient with life itself. "Why was I born? What am I good for?" he asks in torturing uncertainty. He may find relief in religion, or he may merely brood and worry, or he may take the easy road of doubt and skepticism. Because his power to ask questions exceeds the wisdom of the wisest to answer, the absolute mystery of being presses down upon his spirit as if to crush it.

But this creature of intense emotion, and of intense, though narrow, intellectuality, has not corresponding power of action. He can conceive great things, he fancies himself doing great things, but here he stands only less helpless than a child. This is partly because his whole being tends to turn in upon itself and thereby lose the relief that comes from free self-expression. Here, then, are conditions altogether extraordinary. The adolescent can neither continue the free, individualistic, objective life of childhood, nor does he yet perceive how to adjust himself to the larger life. He is likely to become awkward in both body and mind, and the consciousness of this awkwardness may constitute for him a tragedy.

Adolescence, then, is a period of general mental fermentation, but with definite tendencies toward

38

sociality, intellectual independence, a sense of duty and destiny, self-consciousness, and appreciation of the true, the beautiful, and the good. It is evident that childhood religion, like all else in life, will now become yeasty. Indeed, if one's religion is to keep pace with the mental development in other respects, now is the time when religious changes are to be desired as normal incidents in religious growth. To advise an adolescent against religious transformations that shall carry him out of the sphere of his childhood feelings, thoughts, and practices is as vain, and even harmful, as it would be to insist that his childish games and occupations should continue to satisfy.

Adolescence and Religious Awakening.

We shall come near the heart of the matter if we say that the broader, deeper questioning as to the meaning of life, together with the blossoming of the social instinct, brings the need of a new and more deeply personal *realization* of the content of religion. The quickened conscience, with its thirst for absolute righteousness; the quickened intellect, with its thirst for absolute truth; the quickened æsthetic sense, with its intuitions of a beauty that eye hath not seen and ear hath not heard; the quickened social sense, with its longing for perfect and eternal companionship— in short, the new meaningfulness and mystery of life —all this tends to bring in a new and distinct epoch in religious experience. If one has not been religious in childhood, now is the supremely favorable time for conversion; and if one has been religious, there is still need, in most cases, for a personal decision and personal acceptance that shall supersede the more external habits of childhood. Without giving to our terms any theological significance, we may say that conversion, or some equivalent *personalizing* of religion, is a normal part of adolescent growth. This, in fact, is the truth that stands out most prominently as a result of the studies referred to in the Introduction.

To begin with, of 598 miscellaneous cases collected by E. G. Lancaster, 518 showed new religious inclinations between the ages of 12 and 25, and mostly between the ages of 12 and 20.[1] Of 776 graduates of Drew Theological Seminary the largest number were converted at the age of 16, and the average age of conversion was 16.4.[2] Of 526 officers of the Young Men's Christian Associations in the United States and the British Provinces the average age of conversion was almost identical with that of the Drew graduates, namely, 16.5. Furthermore, the average age at which 512 of these officers report that they were *first* deeply affected by religious influences is 13.7.[3] Starbuck found the average age of conversion of 51 men to be 15.7 years, and of 86 women,

[1] *Pedagogical Seminary*, v, 95.

[2] Starbuck, *American Journal of Psychology*, ix, 79.

[3] Luther Gulick, "Sex and Religion," in *Association Outlook* for December, 1897, 54.

13.8 years.[1] He also found a similar change, though less marked than what is ordinarily signified by conversion, occurring in 75 boys at the average age of 16.3 years, and in 120 girls at the average age of 13.7 years. In 110 cases similar to these Lancaster found the average to be, for boys, 15.6 years, and for girls, 14.6.[2]

From my own studies I am able to add the following data:[3] In the first place, judging that what we most desire to know is the *tendency* of these years rather than the outcome, it has seemed to me that what we should look for is not merely conversions, but also awakenings, however these resulted. Accordingly, I have secured a report from 99 men as to their age at each marked religious awakening; that is, at each period of marked increase of religious interest, conviction, etc. These 99 men report 202 awakenings, or an average of two apiece. Distributing these awakenings through the years in which they occurred, from the earliest, at 6 years, up to the age of 28, we get the following table:

Age.	6	7	8	9	10	11	12	13	14	15	16	17	18	19	20	21	22	23	24	25	26	27	28
Number of Awakenings.	1	1	3	3	4	8	19	22	9	13	20	21	14	16	20	6	9	2	3	4	3		1

[1] It is agreed that the adolescent religious change comes with girls a year or two earlier than with boys—a significant evidence of the correlation of the religious with the physical change; for practically the same difference exists in both cases.

[2] Starbuck, *American Journal of Psychology*, ix, 80.

[3] These data were collected chiefly by means of a *questionnaire* which will be found in Appendix A.

These proportions may be graphically represented in the form of the following curve:

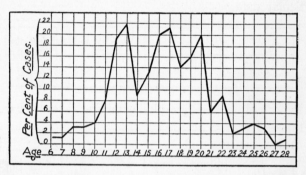

AGE OF RELIGIOUS AWAKENINGS OF 99 MEN.

It is noticeable that there are three well-marked periods of awakening, namely, at 12 and 13, 16 and 17, and 20. Only ten per cent of all the awakenings occurred under the age of 12 years, while fifty per cent occurred at these maximum periods. Again, while ten per cent took place under 12 years, seventy-six per cent fell in the years from 12 to 20. The average age of the men making these reports is 25.4 years. In the entire number there are only three persons under 20, only five under 22, and only eight over 28. The highest age is 36, and the lowest 18. The curve may therefore be regarded as fairly representative for the average age of 25.4 years.

If we now proceed to ask where the *decisive* awakening (conversion, etc.) occurs, we obtain the following results for the 84 cases out of the 99 in which anything decisive could be referred to a particular date:

Age.	7	8	9	10	11	12	13	14	15	16	17	18	19	20	21	22	23	24
Decisive Awakenings.	1	1	1	4	3	8	10	3	7	13	14	6	3	6	1	2		1

Representing these results graphically, as before, this is the curve we obtain:

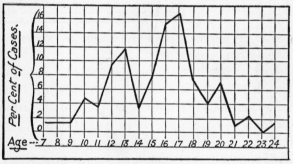

AGE OF DECISIVE RELIGIOUS AWAKENING OF 84 MEN.

The curve goes up at the same points as before, but much higher at 16 and 17 than at any other age. The average age of decisive awakening for the 84 men is 15.4 years, which is only .3 of a year below Starbuck's average, and within 1.1 years of the highest average reached in any group yet reported.

Again, the average age of conversion of 272 members of the Rock River Annual Conference of the

Methodist Episcopal Church is 16.4 years. These conversions are distributed as follows:

Age.	6	7	8	9	10	11	12	13	14	15	16	17	18	19	20	21	22	23	24	25	26	27	28	29	30	31	32	33	34	35	36
Conversions.	1	5	7	9	6	7	23	15	18	20	34	25	18	25	15	13	5	8	4	3	3	1	3		1		1		1		1

Once more platting a curve, we have the following:

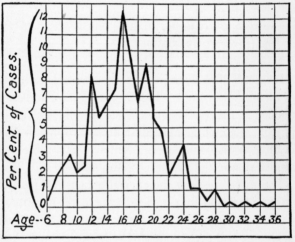

AGE OF CONVERSION OF 272 MEMBERS OF ROCK RIVER ANNUAL CONFERENCE.

Here, as before, the curve shows three crests, and at almost the same points. Furthermore, the average age is 16.4, and the largest number were converted at 16. Ony thirteen per cent were converted under 12, and only sixteen per cent after 20.

Exhibiting in one table the results reached by

examining all these different groups, we have the following very striking statistics:

AGE OF CONVERSION OR DECISIVE AWAKENING OF 1,784 MEN.

	Cases Examined.	Average Age.
Graduates of Drew Seminary	776	16.4
Y. M. C. A. Officers	526	16.5
Starbuck's Conversion Cases	51	15.7
Starbuck's Cases of Spontaneous Awakening	75	16.3
Members of Rock River Conference	272	16.4
My Own Cases of Decisive Awakening	84	15.4
Total	1,784	16.4

If, now, this average age of greatest religious awakening be compared with the age of accession to puberty, the conclusion will be sufficiently convincing that the mental upturning that accompanies the physical transformation is peculiarly favorable to a life decision in the matter of religion.

The three crests of the curves, a fact first pointed out by Starbuck, may also indicate a still closer correlation, namely, between three stages of the physical change and three stages of religious growth.[1] In connection with this point there is an interesting fact about sanctification and similar experiences. My attention having been attracted to the relatively large number of persons who reported having sought or obtained a second experience at about the age of 20, I made definite inquiry on this point. The result is a group of 51 men who experienced what is variously

---

[1] Starbuck, *American Journal of Psychology*, ix, 82.

styled by them sanctification, perfect consecration, etc., this term in every case signifying a more or less definite experience succeeding conversion or the decisive awakening. These experiences are distributed as follows:

Age	13	14	15	16	17	18	19	20	21	22	23	24	25	26	27	28
Second Experience	2	0	0	0	4	4	11	14	4	5	2	2	1	1	0	1

The curve which might be drawn to represent these proportions would give a premonition of itself at 13 (the first period of adolescent awakening), start in again at 17 (the second such period), reach a decided maximum at 20 (the third period), and then rapidly fall away.

All of this goes to show that religious tendencies are a most important feature of general adolescent development. When the approaching change first heralds itself the religious consciousness also tends to awaken. Again, when the bodily life is in most rapid transition the religious instincts likewise come into a new and greater life. Finally, when the fermentation of youth begins to settle into the calmness of maturity, once more religion makes its claim to be counted in the life. It should be borne in mind, of course, that the statistics here presented have been gathered largely from persons under middle age. They do not, therefore, claim to show the average

age of conversion for all Christians. Yet they do show the tendencies of adolescence, and make it probable that something like these results would hold for all large groups.

Interpretations.

Possibly some persons, over-zealous to discredit cherished beliefs, will see in the correlation of religious awakening with physical adolescence an indication that religion or conversion is a product of physical factors. But nothing could well be more illogical than such an inference. What is established is the concomitance of two groups of facts, and this particular instance of such concomitance between mental and physical facts is no more fitted to give comfort to materialism than any other instance of the correlation of brain states with mental states. Let us rather interpret the facts as follows: The mental condition during adolescence is particularly favorable to deep religious impressions. This is the time that the child becomes competent to make a deeply personal life choice; such a choice is now easier than either before or after; this is, accordingly, the time at which a wise Church will expect to reap its chief harvest of members.

The strength of this position is much greater than the statistics alone can reveal. For, even though striking experiences or strong decisions may apparently be lacking, nevertheless, during these same

47

adolescent years, one is likely to experience a new religious attitude, uplift, illumination, or rapid growth. Again, Churches that lay less stress upon the inner experiences and more upon religious nurture place confirmation or a first communion at about the same point in respect to age. And even in these Churches emotional accompaniments are not by any means altogether lacking. It is not uncommon for a Catholic child, for instance, upon partaking of his first communion, to experience emotion so strong that it shines through the face. I am able to state this fact upon the authority of a priest of large experience.

Nor is the Christian religion alone in making this age a turning point. Daniels gives a long list of religious practices signalizing the simultaneous initiation of youths into manhood and into the mysteries and covenants of religion.[1] One of the most beautiful and instructive examples among the North American Indians may be added to Daniels's collection. The custom prevails among many tribes. When an Omaha boy, for instance, arrives at puberty he is sent forth into the wilderness to fast in solitude for four days. To develop self-control, he is provided with bow and arrows, but is forbidden to kill any creature. Arrived on the mountains, he lifts up his voice to the Great Spirit in a song that has been sung under such circumstances from before the time

---

[1] "The New Life," *American Journal of Psychology*, vi, 61ff.

that the white man first set foot upon these shores. The words of the song are, "God! here, poor and needy, I stand!" The melody is so soulful, so appealingly prayerful, that one can scarcely believe it to be of barbarous origin. Yet what miracles may not religious feeling work? The boy is waiting, in fact, for a vision from on high—a revelation to be vouchsafed to him personally and to show what his life is to be, whether that of hunter, or of warrior, or of medicine man, etc. Do you not perceive how the very same impulses sway both the Indian boy and the boy of civilization? Here is the desire to come into *personal* relations with the divinity; here is the facing of ultimate mystery and of destiny; here is the most troublesome problem of youth—that of the life-work.

The religious awakening at this period of life comes in all sorts of ways. Not infrequently it is spontaneous, and altogether independent of revival influences or other pressure from the outside. One young lady relates that, at the age of fourteen, while she was walking in a neighbor's garden, suddenly the thought came to her that she had passed from death to life. There were no especial emotional manifestations, yet this event she has always looked upon as a decisive one. In general, at this age the child's ordinary religious customs and beliefs assume new aspects. They become matters of greater moment, more vitally interesting, more full of feeling.

The ordinary services of the church or the ordinary acts of devotion may become fraught with the most weighty import. In a word, the soil is now prepared for new growth, whether this bursts forth suddenly or whether it makes its appearance in a more gradual fashion. Let us analyze this soil still further.

Religious Feelings of Youth.

Starbuck found fear of death, hell, etc., in only fifteen per cent of his cases,[1] and with this my own results are in striking agreement. They may be conveniently exhibited in the following table of

FEELINGS ACCOMPANYING ADOLESCENT AWAKENING.

	Men.	Women.	Total.
Cases examined....................................	49	24	73
Cases in which fear of God's wrath, of death, hell, etc., is reported in response to specific questions.............	17	3	20
Reporting sorrow for sins known to have been committed..	8	5	13
Reporting general or indefinite sorrow..................	13	2	15
Total number reporting sorrow, overlappings subtracted...	16	5	21

These figures are interesting as respects both fear and sorrow for sin. To begin with fear, it should be noted that in 7 of the cases included in the above table (5 men, 2 women) the fear was distinctly characterized as slight, insignificant, etc. Therefore, the number of cases in which fear played any significant part cannot be more than 13 (12 men, 1 woman), or less than eighteen per cent.

Again, it is evident that the sorrow which these

[1] *American Journal of Psychology*, ix, 281.

youths experienced in their struggles toward the light
was more often an indefinite something than that
which expresses a consciously sinful past. It was
interesting to question the persons from whom these
answers were received as to just what they were
sorry for; and it became more evident than the figures make it that something deeper in us than mere
sorrow for wrong deeds brings to the religious decision. One young man remarks, "I never realized
until after my conversion that I was a rebel against
God." Furthermore, only twenty-seven per cent report any sorrow at all. From this it becomes evident
that, in the case of young persons brought up under
existing religious conditions, the incitements to a religious life are far from being all of a negative sort.

What, then, are the characteristic feelings of an
adolescent when he experiences a religious awakening? For the most part, they are too inarticulate to
be described under any of the ordinary rubrics of
emotion. A mental burden, a sense of unrest, dis-
satisfaction with self, a vague lack, a general discontent, a feeling of wanting something and wanting
to be something that is not clear to one's self—this
comes as near as anything to describing the spontaneous feelings. Of course, if a person who feels
thus is told how to name his feelings, whether as a
sense of sin, burden of guilt, or otherwise, he is likely
to adopt a definite phraseology. But when we secure
careful descriptions we are most likely to find that

the emotions themselves were far less definite than the terms seem to imply. In spite of this misleading tendency in terminology the number reporting fear or sense of sin was very small.

It thus appears that the soil of adolescent religiousness, as far as the feelings are concerned, is an undefined sense of incompleteness, a tantalizing awareness of something as belonging to one's true self, but not yet realized in one's self. In older persons we naturally look for something more definite, but in the case of religiously trained youth like those now under scrutiny such definiteness is not characteristic.

A Hint for the Philosophy of Religion.

We could not, if we would, disguise from ourselves how remarkably these religious feelings mirror the entire physical and mental condition during the middle years of adolescence. The child, as we have seen, is passing into a new state of existence which nothing in his previous experiences enables him to construe in advance. Something belonging to him, yet unknown, is dimly revealing its mysteries. All about him and in him is mystery. He is more than he can understand, yet he apprehends more than he can express. His whole organism, physical and mental, is in a state of unrest, instability, incompleteness. This is the situation. It is a dawn through mists, but such rays as emerge focus themselves in religious longings.

Is there need to utter again the warning that all this is as consonant with a spiritual philosophy as with materialism? Surely the day has passed when a materialistic or any other ontology can be inferred from the assumption that man is a psycho-physical organism. Least of all should they who believe that "the Word was made flesh" stumble at any evidence of correlation between religious phenomena and the phenomena of the bodily life. It has long been recognized and preached that dyspepsia is a foe to religious joy; why, then, should it seem strange that physical adolescence should have its own peculiar correlate in certain tendencies in the spiritual nature? Does not Paul himself teach us that "that is not first which is spiritual, but that which is natural" (that is, animal or sensuous); "then that which is spiritual?" Permit a homely illustration. When it is desirable that the fire in a furnace should burn more briskly we open the draught door, and thereby admit the oxygen which has all along been enveloping the furnace and only waiting for an opportunity to be used in the work of combustion. So the physical changes occurring at adolescence, while they do not produce religion, do, nevertheless, open new doors of impressibility whereby the ever-present divine Spirit may enter the mind and heart more fully than ever before.

Nay, we may even turn to the account of a spiritual philosophy of religion the same facts which seem

at first sight to threaten such a view. For adolescence furnishes a fitting occasion for asking again the
old question, "What is man?" It is now that all the
human capacities are stirred up and come to spontaneous expression. This, then, is a good time for
observing human nature in its simplest forms and
components. What, then, is man? Answer this
question in any way that leaves out the religious
manifestations of arrival at adult life, and you beg
the answer by ignoring the most palpable facts. But
include all the facts, and then you find the conclusion
most natural that man is essentially a religious being,
and that some personal touch with the divine must
be included in complete humanity.

Man is a religious animal just as surely as he is a
social animal; and the possibility of society comes
into being in the closest connection with the new
possibilities of religiousness. The two instincts are,
moreover, curiously blended and interwoven. If it
is obvious that man requires family affection, it is
also manifest that a closely related instinct leads him
on to those higher social relations that culminate in
worship and divine communion.

If there be a heavenly Father who yearns for fel-
lowship with his children, what more effective
method could there be of satisfying that yearning
than to attach to adolescence an appetite for the infinite—the infinitely true, beautiful, and good? As
a matter of fact, such appetite for the infinite is just

the most characteristic mark of mental adolescence. A passion for absolute truth, indubitable certainty, perfect righteousness, all that is most real—this is the mark of it. Then, too, there comes to adolescence a hint of the infinite in the form of beauty. "If I were to spend a day in my own way," writes one just emerging from this period, "I would go off to some beautiful spot where I could be all alone, and there I would try to forget everything that I had left behind, and when it became night I would love to look up into the sky. It seems as though I could see God's perfection there, and make it mine." Sentimental, doubtless; in other words, immature; but the question is a fair one whether life does not grow larger and truth come nearer in proportion as we give scope to these uncorrupted impulses of youth.

55

CHAPTER II

A Study of Some Adolescent Difficulties

I ONCE asked a Catholic priest how he dealt with certain adolescent religious difficulties. His reply showed that he had studied the whole question from the standpoints of physiology, psychology, and heredity, as well as theology, and that he varied his treatment of the cases according to the individual's symptoms. Some persons he controlled simply by authority; others he comforted as a mother soothes a restless infant; still others he sent to a physician. There, thought I, is one who has beheld the ideal of an art of religious culture drawn directly from scientific knowledge. How different is this from the ready-made methods that ignore differences of sex, of age, of disposition, and of physical condition!

He who aspires to be a pastor should doubtless aim to understand and sympathize with the religious difficulties of persons of all ages and conditions. It would be entirely in place to enter a plea for the understanding of childhood, or of mature life, or of old age; but all these are to-day better understood and cared for than the remaining period of life— that of adolescence. Furthermore, when maturity is reached it soon acquires such a stock of experience and such a habit of dealing with its own problems as to differentiate its condition very sharply from that of the awkward and helpless state of youth. Maturity takes an interest in childhood, too, that it strangely withholds from youth. And so, on all accounts, it is that little-understood creature, the youth, whose difficulties have first claim upon the practical psychology of the religious life. That youths of both sexes have many peculiar and characteristic religious embarrassments will be quickly discovered by anyone who secures their confidence sufficiently to know them as they are.

This last remark points to a general difficulty for both the adolescent and his spiritual adviser, namely, the tendency to secretiveness. It is true, no doubt, that youth easily assumes an air of self-sufficiency, independence, even self-assertiveness; but, as often as not, this is a weapon for self-defense adopted by those who do not feel altogether at home or altogether certain of themselves. It is like the air of confidence assumed by an explorer upon meeting a band of savages whose intentions toward him he nevertheless distrusts. The inner self of the youth shrinks from revealing itself, yet it longs to reveal itself if only it can be certain of being understood. Stiff-necked and obstinately self-contained toward all attempts to drive or force it, the heart of youth is nevertheless more docile than that of a child toward one who understands it and is willing to impart to it the guidance that it sorely needs.

Intellectual Difficulties.

As the intellectual difficulties are the ones that come most freely to the surface it is well to begin with them. Let us inquire into the extent and the nature of the perturbing effect of the growing intellectual life upon the religious states of mind. It is noteworthy that several persons of decided intellectual independence report that changes in their doctrinal views have produced little or no effect upon their sense of personal relationship to God; but it is certain that the number who do suffer from this cause, particularly among young men, is very large. Of the persons examined by myself, twenty-three per cent of the men and eight and one third per cent of the women report such troubles growing out of theoretical doubts. Starbuck fixes the average age of the doubt period at about eighteen years for males and about fifteen for females.[1]

It is customary to treat such doubts in one of two ways: either to decry them as a departure or threatened departure from pure religion itself, or else to praise them as an evidence of religious growth. Those who take the former view are content, as a general rule, to exhort the young not to allow anything to loosen their grasp upon that which was delivered to them in childhood. Those who take the more favorable view of doubts, on the other hand, exhort the young to keep their eyes ever open to the rising sun of truth and not to fear any possible effect upon their religious condition. From both sides there sometimes proceed arguments intended to settle the views of the doubter in one way or the other. Thus the everyday treatment of doubts consists chiefly in a very general appeal to the sense of loyalty or to the feeling of independence, together with more or less use of specifically intellectual means.

The defect in most of this procedure lies in the tendency to ignore the depth and extent of the causes of intellectual unrest. What is needed is the psychological point of view in addition to the merely logical and what may be called the merely spiritual. It is necessary to see in the doubt period of youth not merely a perplexed process of reasoning, not merely a weakening of trust or of obedience, but rather a symptom of the entire psychical, yes, and physical, condition at the time. Some sort of intellectual movement and ferment is the natural correlate of the new birth of the physical organism. To see with the eyes of childhood is no longer possible, even if it were desirable. Reconstruction must come in one form or another—the world and life and eternity must all be clothed in new ethical, æsthetic, and intellectual forms. Whether this transformation shall involve the clouding of religious feelings or the relaxing of religious activities depends partly upon childhood instruction, partly upon present conditions and influences.

It is clear, of course, that a child should not be taught anything that he is likely to regard as false as soon as he grows up. The amount of mental agony, not to say religious havoc, wrought by trying to forestall in childhood instruction the questionings that must come to every adult before he has a right to call his opinions his own cannot be measured, but only guessed. "O, why, why," said a young professional man, "did my parents try to equip me with a doctrinal system in childhood? I supposed that the whole system must be believed on pain of losing my religion altogether. And so, when I began to doubt some points, I felt obliged to throw all overboard. I have found my way back to positive religion, but by what a long and bitter struggle!" It requires very little knowledge of the child mind to enable one to perceive that children are simply not yet competent to consider the problems that systems of belief undertake to settle. What appeals as a profound problem to the adolescent, with his wider intimations of the meanings of life, is a mere form of words, or little more, up to that time. In other words, it is simply impossible to provide a child with real solutions of the problems of life. The attempt to do so is doomed to failure in one or more of these directions: either the child is impervious to the attempted instruction, or too early dogmatizing causes an arrest of intellectual development in matters of religion, or the instruction is so misunderstood, and so inadequately understood or so inherently inadequate, that the work will have to be all done over again—possibly with the sweating of blood.

But neither is the adolescent, in the earlier years of this period, quite ready to settle these problems. The moment of taking a plunge into cold water is hardly favorable for making even a guess as to its temperature. Then, too, the tendency to conceit referred to in the last chapter brings in its train a new and peculiar religious difficulty. In most matters the conceit of youth is finally rubbed away by the normal frictions of life. But if that conceit attaches itself to a knowledge of religious dogmas, or a supposed knowledge of them, then the youth assumes the authority of the Almighty in support of his intellectual narrowness and stubbornness. And what is more pitiful in the whole theological world than the imitations of thought that proceed from men thus shut up to prematurity?

It is a recognized pedagogical principle that each branch of instruction should be introduced at just the point where the child's mind has a natural instinct for it. The presence of such an instinct is known by the child's taking an interest in the subject from its intrinsic qualities and not because of extrinsic incitements, and also by a concretely vital as distinguished from merely mechanical or *memoriter* grasp of the subject-matter. Applying this principle to the religious training of children, we

5

THE SPIRITUAL LIFE

should include a great deal of religious activity, but
very little religious theory. The cultivation of religious habits is perfectly feasible, and so is the cultivation of some of the simpler religious emotions.
Facts of religious history will be abundantly assimi-
lated in so far as they are presented in the form of
the story. Thus the whole world of the child may
be filled with what a child can grasp of the divine.
The religious life may be made a natural and joyous
outpouring of his energy, and all without communi-
cating to him the logical basis upon which, possibly,
the parent believes such a life can be justified or demanded. This is, in fact, but another application of
one of the most important truths that dominate the
generation in which we live—the truth that in all
the profoundest practical interests the application of
logic comes *ex post facto;* we do not first discover
the true life by rational processes and then proceed
to live it, but we somehow manage to live the life
that expresses our deepest selves and afterward proceed to see why it is reasonable.

The same principles hold for the adolescent years,
but with a change of application growing out of the
new instincts and points of view that now emerge.
To the child it is possible to say, when difficult theoretical questions come up, "I am not certain," or
"There are differences of opinion on that point;" but
even in the earlier part of adolescence there cannot
be such easy postponement, for the questions are now

becoming real expressions of a budding instinct.
Nevertheless, the youth is almost sure to ask for
more than he can possibly assimilate, and so he is
likely to be contented with much less than he demands. Much of his fever will be allayed if he becomes convinced that his advisers are withholding
nothing from him and yet insisting upon nothing.
What he most wants, after all, is room.

The psychological root of this state of mind is
nothing less than a thirst for the absolute. We shall
presently see that this same thirst manifests itself in
the conscience as a desire for absolute rectitude, absolute self-sacrifice, and all else that belongs to an
absolute ideal. In the sphere of thought its manifestation is a consuming appetite to know the deepest
truth. With this, as a natural corollary, comes a
tendency to dissent and nonconformity. The adolescent feels that no temporizing will do, that authority
is out of place, that uncertainty is torture. Of course,
this attitude marks an immature mind; yet, in the
culture of the religious nature much depends upon
our perceiving that that which seeks to satisfy itself
in this imperious manner is a divine thirst.

Incidentally, it may be worth remarking that
youth's mental aspirations are the very sap of the
tree of knowledge. It is of the utmost value to the
whole cause of truth that the mind, before attaining
the relative fixity of maturity, should for a time assume an utterly free and questioning attitude toward

everything. Without this, religious thought would speedily petrify. Indeed, as soon as thought becomes organized into a system its future growth depends upon its facing henceforth the continuous procession of uncompromising youthful eyes.

We are not, then, to expect intellectual rest and contentment in youth. It is not to be assumed that we can satisfy all the questionings that arise. These questions are life-questions; their solution cannot be put into a formula, but can only be approximated through developing experience. Much—most—that the youth demands to have settled at once can only be lived into as life unfolds its joys and sorrows and aspirations. What, then, can be done for the doubting youth? We can correct the plain misapprehensions under which he is laboring as to what Christians actually believe; we can replace foolish questions with wiser ones; we can guide his reading in the treasuries of the world's thought; we can frankly admit our inability to answer all his questions, and we can tell him that we ourselves have passed through similar difficulties. And we can add to this intellectual food something not less needful; for the trouble of his mind is not merely that he does not know this or that, but rather that he fancies that his uncertainty involves some disloyalty or other fault of heart or of will. He must therefore learn, in a practical way, that knowing Christian doctrine is not the same as being grounded in the Christian life. He should by all means be induced to be active in those forms of religious living that still appeal to him at all. There is, in fact, a fallacy in his reasoning. He fancies that the practical religious life stands or falls according as we accept or reject certain explanations of and reasons for it. But, as before remarked, just the reverse of this is true; the life comes first because it answers to our inarticulate needs, and the fact that it does so answer is sufficient practical justification for its continuance. Hence, religious activity and religious comforts may abide at the same time that the intellect is uncertain of how all this fits into any logical structure. Thus it comes to pass that the greatest thing we can do for the doubting youth is to induce him to give free exercise to the religious instinct. Let him not say what he does not actually believe; let him not compromise himself in any way; but it is always certain that he still believes, feels, and aspires enough to give him a place among religious people.

Furthermore, whenever theoretical doubts become an occasion for pronouncedly morbid states, such as deep worry, melancholy, needless self-condemnation, or fanaticism of any sort, diligent inquiry should be made into the physical condition. When such states are found in young persons of good moral character it is safe to assume that they are less a product of logic than of nerves. Of course, the youth can give what is to him cogent proof why he should worry or fear or be sad, but such reasoning is really little more than a false description of a mere mood. The occasion for it is almost certain to be either some disturbed function, as of digestion, or a general state of nerve fatigue. What is meant by nerve fatigue, how it is commonly induced, and how it is to be treated will demand a section for itself after certain other difficulties have been traced to the same source.

From what has been said it may be concluded that, in order to prescribe for the religious difficulties of the adolescent intellect, one should first respect them because of their deep source and significance. Perhaps the worst calamity that can befall the doubter is not to be understood by those to whom he looks for guidance. What would we say of a doctor of medicine who authoritatively prescribed for a disease that he did not understand? That ought we to think of the unskilled spiritual guide. No process of repression, no mere evasion, not even rigorous logic, will generally suffice. Indeed, it is not unlikely that your callow doubter has hit upon the ultimate mysteries of existence which no theologian or philosopher claims fully to solve. Very likely he has penetrated to real doctrinal difficulties which theologians dispute about among themselves. In any case, that which makes the matter so serious to the doubting youth is a divine discontent with incompleteness which proclaims that we are not mere creatures of time. That he should be strenuous to "know what man and God is" is an advantage and a privilege. His demands cannot be met, of course, but it is possible to give him something greater and better than the most closely woven syllogisms—the sympathy of a sincere soul that has nothing to conceal from him. "Show me the Father," says the youth, "and it will suffice me." The wise friend will reply, as Jesus did, by showing a human self.

The Adolescent Conscience.

We have seen how, when the appetite for the absolute awakens, youth begins to scorn all artificiality and all compromise, and how it turns critic of itself and ofttimes indulges in severe self-condemnation for not attaining the ideal at a bound. Self-exaltation and self-abasement may go hand in hand, the same person being stiff-necked and dictatorial in his relations to others, but a cowering, timid creature in the presence of his own conscience. But the two phenomena have a common root, since he practices toward himself the same intolerance that he shows toward others. He becomes solicitous for both the general principles of a good life and the details of his conduct. Many youths are so fearful of committing the slightest untruthfulness that they studiously preface their statements concerning even the most ordinary matters of fact with some such qualifier as "I suppose," or "I think that." They long to be exactly right, and to know that they are right.

A common form of adolescent casuistry is to assume a major premise expressing some aspect of
duty or of the ideal, and then inquire whether a given
act can, in perfect strictness, be included under it.
There is no end to the self-torment that results. A
girl of twelve had it so impressed upon her mind that
one should never say anything bad about another
that she became afraid to speak of anyone in any way
for fear her words might be wrongly interpreted.
At times, however, she felt called upon to say good
things, even though she knew that they were not
true! The major premise is frequently some accepted maxim, as, "Whatever is worth doing at all
is worth doing well." This is now carried into conduct with absurd intemperance. Thus, a farmer's
son who was running a reaping machine got into the
way of stopping his team and going slavishly back to
pull up every wisp of grain that the machine had
missed. This he did, not for the sake of saving the
grain, but only to preserve intact a certain abstract
ideal of completeness. A girl took a vow, shortly
after her conversion, to pray for the unconverted at
ten o'clock each forenoon. Believing that kneeling
was essential to the fulfillment of her vow, and being
in school at that hour, she had to face the problem of
how to kneel in prayer in the schoolroom among her
fellow-pupils. This is the expedient she adopted:
At ten o'clock each morning she would drop her pen-
cil on the floor underneath her desk, and while in the

act of picking it up would manage to touch her knees to the floor in a momentary prayer!

To us these are trivialities, yet to the youth they seem to contain the very issues of life. And certainly they do express his reverence for some vast and dazzling ideal that has appeared upon his horizon. Not infrequently self-sacrifice or self-annihilation becomes the most beautiful and commanding thing in the world, and so, perhaps, there comes a resolution to be an ascetic or a martyr. I have had young men tell me that when the fact of the brotherhood of men first dawned upon them their warm beds tortured them into sleeplessness through the thought that some of their brothers were cold. Here the trivial and the sublime mingle together; for, though the young man's sleeplessness avails not to solve the ancient problem of the rich and the poor, yet it is precisely because there are always coming to adulthood those who are capable of such feelings that we can hope for progress toward the righting of intrenched wrong.

It is evident that the moral training of youth is a decidedly delicate matter. In the nature of the case, what sufficed for childhood is inadequate. Mere rules, traditions, habits, must be supplemented or even supplanted by personally accepted ideals. Nevertheless, we must not expect mature ideals in those who are in every other way immature. The physical stature of manhood does not imply even physical maturity; much less is it ground for expectation of mature conduct. The very long period of immaturity in the members of the human species is precisely the opportunity which renders possible a superior development of the highest faculties. Awkwardness in conduct must be expected and allowed for. Furthermore, unless immaturity in moral judgment were understood, tolerated, and sympathized with, how could maturity ever be reached? There must be room for free exercise if the muscle is ever to become firm and symmetrical. Try to force upon conduct what the judgment has not approved and you will probably produce revolt toward some extreme that would otherwise be avoided; and even if you succeed, the forcing process may result in a premature stoppage of growth. In the last case you produce the man who never quite makes himself fit into life, however great may be his moral earnestness.

One of the worst faults found in the moral culture of youth is that of treating questions of right and wrong in such a way as to heighten the youthful tendency to hyperconscientiousness. The adolescent conscience can easily be made finical, but how to make it more robust is the real problem. Ofttimes a word is enough to produce a needlessly troubled conscience, to plunge it into the depths of perplexed and unnatural self-examination; but to develop health, which includes at once sensitiveness and equilibrium and vigor,—this calls for moral art. For youth does not easily understand or appreciate that something in childhood which it is the endeavor of our ripest years to win back. It is well expressed in an old motto:

> " Look up and not down;
> Look out and not in;
> Look forward and not back,
> And lend a hand."

It is not self-involution, introspection, self-examination that is needed, but a healthy outward glance, and external interests that call out the best powers. The aim, therefore, should be not so much stimulation as guidance; not so much increased feeling as healthful and absorbing activities; not subjective brooding, but rather a fitting outlet for the mysterious longings that already oppress the heart.

This brings us to the subject of the morbid or hypersensitive conscience in youth, its causes, symptoms, and treatment. Some of its causes, such as wrong advice regarding the point of view, have just been mentioned. But outweighing all others is a physical cause, nerve fatigue. So large a rôle, indeed, does this cause play in the whole spiritual development of youth that it must have a special section.

Religious and Moral Effects of Nerve Fatigue.

Even under the most favorable circumstances the profound character of the adolescent change puts a heavy burden upon the nervous system. This burden may be abnormally increased in many ways, as, for example, too much study, too much indoor life, improper food, too much excitement, irregular habits, private sexual vice, nagging on the part of parents or of teachers, rasping relations at any point. There is ground for a suspicion that the conditions under which a vast majority of adolescents are placed in our modern American life tend to produce a state of habitual fatigue. Among these grounds may be named the tendency to overload the common school and high school curriculum; the amount of social life involving late hours, excitement, and unwholesome eating and drinking permitted to young adolescents, and even expected of them; the multiplicity of interests that crowd out simplicity and repose, and, finally, the almost feverish intensity with which American youth, at least, enter into their too varied occupations. It would scarcely be an exaggeration to assert that sixteen-year-old girls and eighteen-year-old boys are expected to live two lives in one— the life of students and the life of men and women of the world. We all know what this leads to in those whose powers of resistance are under the average, or whose scholarly or social ambitions lead them into more than the ordinary expenditure of vital energy. But the results of this set of conditions do not stop with the young persons who break down. The others also meet the nemesis of nature just as surely, though not so obviously. The consequences enter into the whole life, and may end only with the life. Let us notice briefly how moral and religious interests are affected.

For our purposes the essential characteristic of a fatigued nerve is its increased irritability; it reacts to less than the normal stimulus, and hence more or less spasmodically. For example, in a state of fatigue one is more likely to start at small noises; furthermore, one's reaction is likely to be ill-directed, uncertain, prolonged. Let the same cause produce its natural effects in the workings of the intellect, the feelings, and the will, and we shall have, among other things, an important group of morbid moral and religious states. The following may be enumerated as examples: worry, despondency, bad temper, emotionalism of various kinds, oversensitiveness, lack of decision in small matters, morbid introspection, hyperconscientiousness, increased susceptibility to temptations of appetite and of sex. The discussion of what are called temptations will be postponed to the next section. Our present interest is to notice the influence of fatigue in producing morbid or hyperconscientiousness.

Just where normal sensitiveness of conscience leaves off and abnormal begins cannot always be stated with certainty in particular cases, but in general when the sense of right and wrong is so intense as to defeat instead of promote proper conduct we are safe in calling the conscience morbid. Conscience is morbid when trifles are magnified into monsters, when debate with one's self as to what is right is carried to the point of self-blinding or of paralysis of decision, and, in general, when anxiety about right-doing exhausts the energy that ought to go into moral action. Then

> " the native hue of resolution
> Is sicklied o'er with the pale cast of thought;
> And enterprises of great pith and moment
> With this regard their currents turn awry,
> And lose the name of action."

Here are a few examples that have come directly under my notice:

A girl is so tortured by uncertainty as to what she was created for that she lays aside her usual occupations and refuses for months to see her friends. Others feel so keenly the demand for absolute accuracy and completeness that the main purpose of action is defeated by their slavish attention to preliminaries or to details. Thus the youth already referred to as being too particular in running his father's reaper adds the following items from his experience: "If, in plowing corn, I missed a weed, I could not bear to leave it, and so, often got off the plow and, going back, pulled it up. Sometimes I became angry instead of going back, and then vented my rage on the horses, thinking that they had not walked as they should. Likewise in running a self-binder. I worked myself nearly to death changing the machine for 'up' and 'down' grain in order that *every* scrap should be gotten, and that every bundle should be bound *just a trifle* nearer the 'butts' than the heads. [Italics are in every case his own.] If the horses went into the grain, thus causing the machine to run over some and leave it, I often went back and pulled it up, not to save it, but 'just for the looks of the thing.' I wanted everything to run *absolutely perfectly*, and if it did not I was perplexed and fretted."

Later, when the same young man was preparing for college, he neglected his health and his religious and social life, as he says, "all for the sake of being *extremely* accurate in unimportant details in geometry, Latin, and Greek. Also, in writing essays, I have rewritten many pages rather than scratch out a misplaced dot or wrongly crossed 't.' During these two years in no essay did I ever scratch out with a knife or otherwise *anything*, no matter how small, and *never* put in a word with a caret. If I made a mistake I rewrote the whole page. . . . Practically, after the age of nineteen I was not troubled with morbid conscientiousness."

Attention may be called to three things in this account: First, the close affinity between this form of morbid conscientiousness and anger. It is a case of what is popularly called "nerves." That is, the nervous system, through the great tax placed upon it

in this period of life and through contributory causes,
such as special fatigue and inadequate nutrition, is
in unstable equilibrium, and ready upon trifling
stimuli to tumble over either in the form of anger,
or of excessive feeling, or of motor discharges disproportionate to the occasion. Second, notice that
oversensitiveness of conscience coalesces with "showing off," thus revealing very clearly the sociological
significance of the whole phenomenon. The boy was
overparticular, not to save the grain, but "just for
the looks of the thing." This is the startled response
of one who hears for the first time the voice of the
race speaking within him. Third, notice the exaggeration of details, and the effort to reach the absolute in conduct. Everything is now put into one
formula, "either—or." Nothing but the absolutely
perfect is right; all else is wrong. The call of conscience comes to him in the form of law, pure and
simple. Morality is as yet abstract and lacking in
content. He has not yet grasped the notion of
growth or becoming, nor seen that benevolence is
the fulfilling of the law. Right here, no doubt, lies
the root of much of the youth's anguish. The full
authority of duty,

" Stern Daughter of the Voice of God,"

presses down upon his spirit; but it is a yawning
emptiness which he seeks to fill by infinite yearnings
and by absurd slavery to trifles.

76

The analysis of this case will apply in large degree to many others. For instance, a girl of about a dozen years was plagued with overnice conscientiousness about stealing. She would not take so much as a pin without permission, or if when visiting any of her friends she found it necessary to take one, she inflexibly compelled herself to tell the hostess, saying, "I took one of your pins." This was a very painful process to her, though she did not see the absurdity of it, but thought she was merely doing her duty. She had a similar overwrought sense of the duties of politeness. She says: "On one occasion a neighbor took me into her flower garden to pick me a bouquet. As she picked each flower she put it into my hand, and each time I said, 'Thank you.' I was greatly embarrassed, but a sense of duty compelled me to keep on offering my gratitude for each separate flower, until finally the lady assured me that it was not necessary."

As one grows older, one is likely to become aware of the unreasonableness of such a conscience, yet may not be able to resist its commands. A young lady writes: "I have suffered at intervals ever since I can remember from what I consider to be a morbid conscience. However, my training has always been of such a healthy sort that now I seem to be outgrowing this tendency, and abnormal conscientiousness crops out only when I am in considerable physical fatigue. . . . The reason why I call these spasms of conscience morbid is because they seem to be a distinct hindrance instead of a help in doing what I believe to be right. I want to do right, my ideal of the right is very high, but with it all is a terrible sense of self-distrust. Instead of guiding self in the performance, conscience seems to dissipate, to scatter, all self's energy. This waste of energy is immense, and the results painful. The last attack of this sort was when I was trying to write [a certain literary production]. I had an idea which I wished to develop and express as well as possible. But the thoughts that arose were condemned as petty, as unworthy. The words that flowed from my pen were despicable. The structure seemed miserably weak. Decision, even on the most minute points, was well-nigh impossible. The experience was altogether painful, and the struggle nearly fruitless; and all through it I was aware that it was abnormal; but that did not seem to help matters. I was overworked at the time. I should advise a good ten-hour sleep as a cure for, or insurance against, attacks of this sort. I have always been extremely sensitive even of little frowns of disapproval, and from them have suffered cruelly as a child. This, I believe, is a mild case of morbid conscience."

In this case, which is doubtless typical of a large class, the sufferer is not deceived at all, but recognizes the fact that her feeling of right and wrong has become distorted. Another important fact here is the clear indication of the connection between morbid conscientiousness and fatigue. "I now," says the writer, "seem to be outgrowing this tendency, and abnormal conscientiousness crops out only when I am in considerable physical fatigue." The last attack came on when she was overworked. We might even say that fatigue, however induced, is the neural basis of morbid conscientiousness. Our experience in mature life witnesses to this fact. For when we are tired out we are often brought into a sort of slavery to our duties, and especially to details; we are drawn in so many different directions that we do not know which way to turn, and we seem incapable of getting any task quite done. Under these circumstances small matters unduly excite us, even when we are fully aware that there is no good reason for our agitation. With adolescents this condition may become habitual and all-absorbing. The victim becomes a slave of indecision. He sees considerations on both sides of every question of conduct, is harassed by fear of deciding for the wrong side, and often ends by letting slip the opportunity for action. Then comes, perhaps, remorse and mental flagellation for his weak and vacillating character. One young man says: "I was troubled for several years by a lack of prompt decision, especially in small matters. If once I got to arguing with myself over a thing, I was likely to argue too long, and small emergencies were often too much for me. I derived the greatest help from learning to ride the bicycle when

I was twenty years old, for in bicycle riding I found prompt and accurate decisions necessary, and apparently forced out of me."

This lack of decision is closely akin to certain incipient approaches to fixed or insistent ideas. A young lady who was much troubled in her early teens by an oversensitive conscience tells me that, on one occasion, having been deeply impressed by the suicide of a neighbor, she conceived an overwhelming fear that she might kill her mother. It brought her into sharp anguish of mind for some days, when she found relief by confiding the trouble to her mother. A young man who from the advent of puberty to the age of twenty-five suffered from three distinct and serious attacks of nervous exhaustion, and each time endured torments from his conscience, experienced in one attack at least something approaching insistent ideas. As he walked along the street he felt that he must touch every post of the fence and not step on any crack in the sidewalk; and these were not mere passing whims, as they frequently are in childhood, but commanding ideas which wrung obedience out of him against his own judgment. The same youth had a consuming fear of hydrophobia. Something of the same sort is found in persons who lock and relock the door several times at night, being unable practically to convince themselves that they have already completed this duty. Such a person, though intellectually convinced of the folly of his acts, feels impelled to rise from bed again and again and examine the door lest he may possibly have made a mistake the other times. I have found this phenomenon present in many adolescents.

In some cases absolute consistency is the rub. There may be no lack of decision—rather precipitateness of decision growing out of narrow ideas of right. Thus, a youth who was singing in a church choir had doubts on doctrinal points. Consequently, whenever, in the singing of a hymn, he came to a passage that he could not accept as his own belief he refused to sing it. Faithful to his misunderstanding of duty, he finally left the choir on this account.

Again, conscience often becomes morbid over the question of one's lifework. Myriads of adolescents worry and weep over the problem of what they are good for, and whether they ought not to become missionaries, or at least ministers. Concerning this group of cases two remarks may be of service. In the first place, many, perhaps most, of these struggles occur where the intention to do right already exists. They are therefore less a fight between a defined selfish motive and a defined unselfish one than a mere floundering about in the confusion wrought by self-distrust. I have known young men to hestitate to follow their common sense lest selfish motives might have corrupted even that. In such cases the defect is not selfishness, but rather an overrefinement, or

double distillation, of unselfishness. It is an unself-
ing that paralyzes both judgment and will.

A second remark concerning this lifework fever
is that there is often a tendency to decide upon the
ministry, or missionary work, or some heroic occupation, simply and solely through confusion between
the form and the content of duty. We have seen
that youth is a time when the absoluteness of the
moral imperative strongly overawes the mind; that
self-sacrifice now becomes beautiful, and that a longing may arise to annihilate one's self for some glori-
ous cause. If, now, there already exists a firm notion
that the ministry or any other occupation is a peculiarly unselfish one, the oversensitive conscience may
at once interpret its acute desires for righteousness
as a call from high heaven to this particular work.
Thus, through confusion produced by mere association of ideas, a particular occupation becomes identified with the form or imperativeness of duty itself.
The reasoning is this: I ought to live a wholly unselfish life, therefore I will be a minister.

What has just been said is not a guess at the truth,
but a report of fact. A young man, for example,
who was obviously ill-adapted for the ministry, and
who, on the other hand, felt strong moral drawing
toward another field of usefulness, was nevertheless plagued with a feeling that he ought to be a
minister. He consulted a person older than himself,
and received this advice: "Possibly what you take

to be a call to the ministry is rather a call to completeness in your consecration. Go and settle this latter question first, and ask yourself whether you are equally willing to serve God as a business man or as a minister." After several weeks the youth returned and announced his conviction that he had been called to divine service as a business man.

Right here, in psychological misunderstandings, I am convinced, lies one explanation of the tenacity with which unadaptable, stupid, or otherwise inefficient men insist that they are called of God to preach the Gospel. Perhaps the most striking experience in their entire moral history has been a morbid anxiety about their lifework. Having no means of guessing that it is morbid, they interpret it as the divine Spirit tugging at their wills and soliciting them to preach.

We hear a great deal in these days about a dearth of able preachers. May it not be that the grade is being kept low, first, by our placing too much confidence in the subjective, individual impressions of candidates who, instead of being really called, are simply suffering from the consequences of nerve fatigue; and, second, by our failure deliberately to solicit and guide toward the ministry the young men whom the Churches judge to be strongest in the requisite qualities? It is surely allowable to suppose that the divine will with respect to the ministry may be made manifest through a careful use of enlightened judgment. Furthermore, is there any valid reason why we should not suggest to the right kind of young men that their possession of the gifts itself constitutes a call?

Trouble of conscience over one's personal religious status is another form of morbidness. It is very common in Churches that put much stress upon assurance, or the witness of the Spirit. I find this phenomenon present in the history of forty per cent of the young men and forty-four per cent of the young women whose reports I have in my possession. Some of these reports reveal an almost tragic amount of suffering on this point. Certainly in some cases the trouble was not merely unfortunate teaching, but also an unfortunate condition of the nervous system. Not infrequently such a period of religious unrest coincides with a period of obvious ill health. I have before me an account of a young girl who became a mental and physical wreck with the delusion in her head that she had committed the unpardonable sin. This girl had always been very nervous and very religious. She was finally rescued by a woman who cured her by faith. The correlation of doubts with ill health is apparent, also, in the following account from a young man: "I must have been about twelve years old when I had, as I supposed, a religious change, and joined the Church. From that time for about five years I was continually in a state of unrest and trouble, magnifying, as I now think, perfectly innocent things into sins of the deepest dye.

And, as I tried to bind myself down to a perfectly correct course and, as a matter of fact, failed, I was continually in a state of remorse, and also continually thinking of myself and my acts, till I came to be almost unbearable to myself. When about eighteen I was taken sick. . . . After my recovery I had lost all the supersensitiveness."

But not merely in states of positive ill health are these doubts of one's personal religious status to be found. They are liable to be found wherever religious teachers have induced young persons to practice a spiritual barometry and thermometry upon themselves. Of course, however, the weed grows most rank where the power of resistance of the nervous system is lessened by fatigue. As maturity approaches, and power consequently ripens, the doubts can be, and are frequently, banished by an act of will. The following account is fairly representative of a considerable class of persons: "When I was about twelve years old I began to assume the outward forms of a religious life. I met all the conditions of being a Christian as far as I understood them, and at fourteen joined the Church. But from about this time until I was twenty I was constantly haunted by the thought that I did not know for sure whether I was a Christian or not. I prayed, and read the Bible, and struggled bitterly with my secret doubts, though I hardly mentioned them to anyone else. There were times when it seemed to me that I would walk into the fire if such torture could cure my mental agony. But all in vain. At last I became ashamed and disgusted, and decided that, having done my duty as far as I knew how, I would not be bothered any more. That ended it."

Is it not monstrous that sensitive souls who have loyally dedicated themselves to God should be permitted, through causes within our control, to suffer this purgatory of doubt whether God accepts the offering?

In all the sorts of morbidness here described three distinct causes are likely to contribute each its share: First, the general yeastiness of the mind at the time of the change from childhood to adulthood; second, unwise teaching, or lack of wise teaching; third, an overburdened nervous system. This general subject might have been discussed with propriety under any one of these heads. If I have seemed to place religious and moral difficulties in unusually close proximity to physiology, it is because of a conviction that untold spiritual treasure is slipping from our hands simply because we forget that religious states, as well as other states of mind, stand in a reciprocal relation with states of the brain and nervous system. Furthermore, there has long prevailed—when, indeed, was it otherwise?—a habit of trying to control effects without controlling causes. It is so easy to scold, or to exhort one to have trust, or to reason out how one *ought* to feel, but so hard to get at the actual causes of our states, that we allow ourselves to choose the smoother path.

But perhaps enough has been said to show the necessity of tracing religio-moral difficulties to their causes, and to indicate what some of those causes are. All of which ought to cast at least a little light upon the functions of the wise parent or other religious guide. For such a guide to add to any existing irritability by laying still heavier burdens upon the conscience, by multiplying the doubts, by adding blacker hues to the outlook upon life—this is next thing to crime. And this is precisely what may be done by telling a young person to examine his heart frequently; or by painting before him the rigors of the moral law without equal emphasis upon the beauty of the moral ideal; or by appealing to his fears; or by describing his duties and privileges as though there were no difference in capacity between him and a mature person; or by telling him that doubt is sin, and that life is a continual fight with snakes in the grass. The victim of such teaching may be religious, but he is pretty certain to be spiritually deformed also. What religion ought to do for youths is not to increase their already overdriven subjectivity, but to restore it to equilibrium with objective interests. And not only does wrong teaching deform the moral-religious nature, it also tends to injure the body itself. For the relation between body and mind is reciprocal. One young man, in his report of his experience, insists that a period of two years of physical distress was induced directly by excessive religious irritation.

The surest way to control these difficulties is, first, through physical hygiene and, in some cases, medical treatment. Nutritious but not stimulating food, proper regulation of the digestive system, plenty of sleep and of fresh air—these have direct spiritual value. Then comes mental hygiene; that is, mental occupations and exercises that take the attention from self and send it out toward free and joyous associations and activities. Especially necessary is a life of cheerful, but not too intense or excessive, activity. This last grows out of the fact, before noticed, that the will of the adolescent is less developed than the feelings and the intellect. It is from this weakness of will that arises much of his feeling of being pent up, of being shut off from life, of having no outlook upon the world. What is needed here is training in self-expression, and this can be promoted by wise guidance of the mental and physical powers —the mental powers largely through hearty, unconstrained social intercourse, the physical powers through games and athletic exercises as well as through work.

Finally, greater than all else is sympathy. Nothing, indeed, can be a substitute for a personality that appreciates all that the youth feels but cannot understand. These neophytes, entering with fear and trembling upon their initiation into manhood and womanhood, do not ask our pity, but they do need to get acquainted with us so as to find out how grown persons feel and think and act. Once more, it is the revelation of humanity, which is the revelation of divinity, that heals the woes of the world.

Psychological Aspects of Certain Temptations.

What are the most common moral struggles of youth? Apparently a bad temper heads the general list. Next, in the case of males, comes difficulty with the sexual nature—a struggle for wholesomeness of both mind and body. To discuss either of these darker features of the young life about us is not an agreeable task. But, if we ask what is useful rather than what is pleasant, we shall agree that the moral and spiritual guides of youth should not shrink from fully understanding the nature and causes of the evils which they seek to remedy or to prevent.

How, then, shall we understand bad temper? If possible, let us secure a psychological view of the facts as distinguished from all popular or theological theories of the relation of this fault to depravity, moral law, and the responsibility that grows out of freedom. Let us admit, what is very fact, that our self-knowledge is not sufficiently developed to enable us to tell with accuracy just what measure of freedom may be exercised in any single act. It is undoubtedly possible to indulge ill temper by what has every appearance of being the most fully voluntary choice. Yet this is not the rise of ill temper, but only the encouragement of it or the refusal to suppress it. Granted, then, that through our voluntary attitude toward it it may become habitual, or even a matter of disposition, we still need to know how the thing itself originally springs into being.

Again, psychology can neither affirm nor deny that there may be in all temptation some influence from Satan or other evil spirits. Our observation does not extend so far. As for depravity, to which in other days all the angers of even infancy were ascribed, we shall at this point assume no positive attitude whatever. We may remain psychologically noncommittal all the more easily because it plainly appears that the psychology of temptation is the same whatever our theory of depravity may be. Thus, if by depravity we mean some taint of the soul, we shall expect it to manifest itself only in particular acts which have definite correlations with brain functions, as well as with other mental states. On the other hand, if by depravity we mean that something of the beast remains in us because of our evolution from lower forms of life, the modes of its manifestation will still be the same.

It must be frankly admitted, nevertheless, that when we view the facts from the psychological and the evolutionary points of view the very problems which theories of Satan and of depravity try to solve assume a new meaning, or even tend to lose their meaning. Theoretically it is always possible to find room in our ignorance of details for any desired kind of factor; yet practically we find the problem shifting, and we tend to finish our study without caring to answer all the questions that may have been uppermost at the beginning.

Ill temper is simply a misapplication of a useful and even necessary function. This is sometimes expressed by saying that temper is as necessary to a man as it is to a steel tool, but that evil arises when temper is uncontrolled. Another popular expression of the same thing, and an amusing one, too, is the distinction often made between anger and "righteous indignation." Of course this distinction of names is adhered to simply for the sake of saving a theory—the theory, namely, that all anger is sinful. Now, a moment's self-analysis will show that "righteous indignation" is nothing but righteous anger. Jesus exhibited intense anger of this kind, and if he had not done so one perfection would have been lacking from his portrait. It seems strange that so obvious a fact should have had so little recognition in popular religious instruction. For surely, when everybody knows that the merely yielding, accommodating, passive, pulpy character is utterly one-sided, it is next to suicidal for the Church to represent Jesus as lacking in aggressiveness and without passionate devotion to his principles.

Considered in respect to its origin in the animal kingdom, anger is simply feelingful opposition to that which is injurious. It is the psychological part of the struggle for self-preservation. This simple aspect of it may be witnessed through a large part of the scale of animal life. Long before evolution reaches man, however, anger assumes a second aspect, an altruistic one. A parent bird, for instance, may show the most unmistakable signs of anger when her nest is approached; a bear breaks into the most awful passion against any supposed enemy of her cubs. With man, finally, this altruistic aspect becomes broad enough to appear as the most feelingful opposition to whatever threatens or opposes universal good. In other words, with man the function of anger, which was first simply a part of the machinery for self-preservation on the part of various animals, is capable of being transfigured into an engine for the realization of the highest ideals.

We can now see how to differentiate between the anger that is to be suppressed and prevented and that which is to be cherished as one of man's noblest attributes. Anger is good when it promotes the highest ideal, the brotherhood of man. This implies all that is essential for prompt and effective self-preservation and for prompt and effective defense of others against nefarious designs. A father, for instance, who should be summoned to defend his daughter against the assaults of a brutish man would be lacking in moral fiber if he were not enraged with the criminal. It must not be forgotten that, though reason is necessary to guide the ship of life, feeling is the steam that propels it.

On the other hand, anger is bad whenever it operates against the realization of the ideal of brotherhood. It is dangerous whenever it controls the man instead of being controlled for moral ends. Subordinate manifestations of such anger are impatience, "touchiness," and undue vehemence of feeling toward the persons or things that one dislikes or disapproves. We have now to ask after some of the chief conditions under which these various harmful states arise.

Nerve fatigue is the key to the understanding of spontaneous tendencies to irritable temper. In fact, touchiness and spasmodic acts of all sorts are the exact psychical counterpart of the state of a worn nerve. To see that this is true one needs only to ask one's self whether anger occurs more commonly in the morning or in the afternoon; more often after a sound night's rest or after sleepless hours; more often during the hour before dinner or during the hour after dinner; more often when the digestion is good or when it is bad. From these considerations it will become plain that it is the overworn or underfed nerve that furnishes one of the chief conditions of ill temper. Hence the justification for the oft-repeated assertion, "I was not myself when I said that." Now, just so far as such conditions of the nerves are unavoidable, blame for the tendency to irritability is unreasonable. Under such circumstances one may always say, with Paul: "The good that I would, I do not: but the evil which I would not, that I do. Now if I do that I would not, it is no more I that do it, but sin that dwelleth in me." But, while we extenuate unavoidable tendencies to ill temper, we must not forget that, the chief cause being known to be a physical state largely under our own control, our responsibility is by no means slight. What is perfectly clear is that we should treat this fault chiefly by removing its causes.

Again, physical and mental hygiene (see page 88) contain the desired leverage. Instead of scolding, or doing anything else to cause youths to agonize over their ill temper and so add to the tension and fatigue of their nerves, we would better say to them: "This is not as bad as you imagine. Your anger is sinful only as far as you voluntarily indulge it or voluntarily neglect the means to prevent and overcome it. Unless you do employ some effective means for gaining self-control the trouble will become deep-seated and chronic; but the means are simple enough." Then should follow exhortations not only to trust in the help from on high, but also to take the hygienic measures, both physical and mental, to which reference has just been made.

Much that has been said about ill temper applies,

word for word, to the temptations arising directly from the fact of sex. The discussion of this momentous topic with anything approaching adequacy would require a special monograph. Yet, when Starbuck finds that about a third of the males whose religious experience has been communicated to him give sexual temptations as the most prominent ones in youth,[1] it becomes obvious that the topic cannot be altogether omitted in any discussion of temptations. In my own studies I have not sought for revelations of experience on this point, yet a considerable proportion of the young men found it necessary to mention such temptations in order to make their religious experience clear to me; in many other cases it was plain that the same sort of temptations were referred to under some more general name. It is perfectly clear that the most serious source of religious difficulty for adolescent males lies precisely in sexual irritability. In other words, as in the case of anger, so here, what we have to understand is, first and foremost, certain forms of heightened or abnormal irritability of the nerves.

This is, perhaps, as good a place as any to say that a puny, "spirituelle" body, the body that many of the saints have aspired to have, gives no advantage in the struggle with the carnal nature. Perhaps it is true that the strongest passions are most likely to be found residing in a robust body, but a more impor-

tant truth is that the possession of such a body is a
condition most favorable to self-control. Anyone
familiar with the lives of the saints knows that the
austerities with which they hoped to conquer their
carnal nature were a failure. The impoverished state
of the nervous system that resulted from fasting,
vigils, overstudy, and all the other ascetic devices
made desire more active, if anything, and at the same
time weakened the natural inhibitions. Besides, the
very occupation of seeking to escape sin by with-
drawing from a rounded, healthy life fixed the
thoughts with all the greater intentness upon the
ideas that were best calculated to tempt. Applying
this to our present problem, we may say at the outset that the two great conditions that we should seek
to establish and maintain with boys and young men
are these: a thoroughly robust physical life and a
mind fully occupied with wholesome thoughts.
These are, of course, large requirements, and many
things may help or hinder their realization; but a
few very simple and plain as well as influential means
are at the disposal of every parent who cares to pro-
tect his sons.

In the first place, since, as soon as puberty approaches, curiosity may fix the attention upon matters of sex until it acts as an irritant, the general
nature of sex should be explained long before that
time. Another evil that this course will tend to prevent is the uncleanness with which matters of sex

are sure to be associated in any mind that learns them surreptitiously or by chance. It is sometimes argued that the simplicity of the child mind should not be disturbed by early information upon such matters. This view, however, ignores two facts: first, that the necessary information can be so communicated as not to disturb this simplicity. If properly communicated, the knowledge will be taken much as other prosaic, everyday facts. This is the testimony of parents who have loved their children enough to be frank in answering their questions. The other fact which this specious argument ignores is that children do obtain information regarding sex, if not from their parents, then from playmates, servants, or even by observation. What a ridiculous kind of delicacy is that which refuses to satisfy the curiosity of children in a pure and delicate manner when the alternative is that the information will be acquired with possibly many foul mental associations! Perhaps the most judicious point of view from which to treat the subject is that of biology. The law of sex can be traced up from the flowers to the domestic animals and man as a mere scientific fact, without the first suggestion of indelicacy. Again, adequate specific knowledge of the dangers of this period of life should be imparted before experimentation or vile companions have a chance to turn a danger into a reality. It is probable that bad habit starts oftener in curiosity and ignorance than in any other way, and this danger is certainly one that parents can counteract.

Adolescents should be made to understand that there is a reciprocal relation between the mental condition and the physical condition. They should be warned of the physical consequences of impure thought, and so of listening to or telling what is not strictly wholesome. They should at the same time be made aware that the temptation to impure thoughts has often a physical basis. Great ignorance exists here among those who need knowledge. On the one hand, the difference is not clearly seen between a tempting thought and a sinful thought. Jesus was explicit in making the sin to consist in *indulging* the impure suggestion (Matt. v, 28). On the other hand, it is not sufficiently recognized that suggestions of evil come chiefly through physical conditions that are largely under one's control. Whatever produces either general or special nerve irritability tends in the wrong direction.

Thus, once more, we are confronted with nerve fatigue as a most important key to adolescent difficulties, and with physical and mental hygiene as the most important preventive and remedy. It sometimes gives heart to struggling youths merely to tell them that their temptations are not evidence of badness, but rather an incident of a period of growth or of temporary and controllable conditions of the nervous system. Furthermore, if parents or other advisers are to succeed in controlling or guiding at all, they must understand the timidity of youth and must find ways to establish confidential relations in spite of it. Youths who dare not ask questions or seek advice from their natural advisers are thrice defenseless. They are more liable to temptation, less equipped against it, and in danger of becoming victims of the robbers and murderers who advertise to help. It is a strange commentary upon the supposed superior modesty of American life that the only persons to whom thousands upon thousands of youths dare confide their questions or their difficulties are quacks who line their pockets largely by promoting the very evil which they pretend to cure.[1]

If the question be asked, Whose place is it to assume the responsibility for this part of the training of the young? the answer is that this is emphatically

---

[1] Parents who desire to know what to teach their boys will find the following publications worth a reading. As a general rule, printed matter on this subject would better not be put into the hands of young adolescents. The element of personal sympathy and acquaintance is indispensable. In the later years of the adolescent period, however, some brief and judicious printed statements are in place :

Burt G. Wilder, Professor in Cornell University : *What Young People Should Know*. Pp. 212. Boston, Estes and Lauriat, 1875. $1.50.

L. B. Sperry : *Confidential Talks with Young Men*. Pp. 179. Revell, 1893. 75 cents. *Confidential Talks with Young Women*. Pp. 160. Revell, 1895. 75 cents.

Grant Allen : *The Story of the Plants*. Pp. 213. Appleton, 1897.

Mary Wood-Allen : *Almost a Man*. Pp. 36. 25 cents. *Child-Confidence Rewarded*. Pp. 19. 10 cents. *Teaching Truth*. Pp. 24. 25 cents. Wood-Allen Pub. Co., Ann Arbor, Mich.

Margaret Warner Morley : *A Song of Life*. Pp. 155. McClurg, 1891. $1.25. *Life and Love*. Pp. 214. McClurg, 1895. $1.25.

Earl Barnes : " Feelings and Ideas of Sex in Children," *Pedagogical Seminary*, vol. ii, p. 199.

The above titles are taken from the *Association Outlook* for June, 1898.

7/32

the work of parents. Nevertheless, in view of the awful neglect of parents, it is worth considering whether pastors and school-teachers will not feel themselves forced, as soon as they realize the situation, to assume some responsibility. If possible, they should reach the children by imparting to the parents the needed knowledge and moral impulse. But, in one way or another, those who perceive where lies the greatest moral and religious difficulty of adolescent boys and young men have the opportunity of doing a service to humanity and religion that is of the very first importance.

The Natural History Method of Handling Moral and Religious Difficulties.

It would not be strange if some readers missed in the present chapter what they regard as essential in the treatment of any practical problem of the religious life. Has not the divine element been ignored, and has not the whole discussion proceeded as if the distinction between body and soul, hygiene and spirituality, physiology and theology, had been obliterated? For reply, one might retort with a query whether religious instruction and training has not, as a general rule, been blind to some of the most obvious conditions of a healthy spiritual life; whether, by ignoring the relation of physiology and of psychology to spiritual culture, it has not failed to control large sections of the man, thus leaving spirituality attenuated and one-sided; whether, finally, despite has not thereby been done to an essential and profound Christian principle concerning the realization of the spiritual in and through the natural. Instead of discussing the question in the form of charge and countercharge, however, it is better to give a plain statement of the relation of our natural history method to the conception of a spiritual life under the immediate control and guidance of the divine Spirit.

In the first place, let it be said that our discussion does consciously and intentionally assume the falsehood of all purely ascetic views of the nature and ends of religion. Instead of forbidding, a normal religious life involves the proportionate exercise, under fitting conditions, of all the functions with which nature has endowed the whole human being. Its end is not to deliver man from the life that now is, but to manifest and actualize within that life the divine ideal. The religious man seeks to make his whole life an incarnation—a living of the divine life here and now, in the whole network of interlaced mental and physical activities. Whether he eats or drinks, or whatever he does, he does all so as to glorify God. Thus and only thus can he carry forward the work of the incarnation—in-fleshing—to which Christianity traces its origin. That for which the present chapter pleads, then, is simply the reinstatement of the body in its original place of honor in the Christian view of life. When it advises attention to physical hygiene as a condition of a healthy spiritual life it implies no theory not already recognized and accepted in the doctrine that the Word was made flesh.

What would be the consequences of putting this view into practice? If in our eating and drinking, our sleeping and waking, our work and our play, we saw only religious acts; if we perceived that normal functions tend to pleasure as abnormal ones to pain, and that all normal functions belong to religion, what would be the effect upon our religious joy? Would religion be more or less attractive and influential over the lives of men? To ask these questions is to answer them. When every science that has to do with the life that now is comes to be regarded as showing the way to the life that is divine, then, indeed, the religion of incarnation will come to its own.

But how about the divine or supernatural element in the religious life? What has natural history to do with God's government of his moral universe? Is it not prayer that we need, rather than psychology? Perhaps prayer *and* psychology, but certainly not the kind of praying that expects God to do for us what we can do for ourselves. Would it not be grotesque to believe in God as the creator of our whole being and yet imagine that we dishonored prayer to him by seeking to understand all sides of

that being so as to control them all for his glory?
We might even ask whether this latter is not itself
as real a kind of prayer as any.

All this line of thought is so obvious that further
pursuit of it may be dispensed with. What has been
said will not be in vain, however, if it only stimulates
to reflection upon the recognized principles of our
religion. Among these consequences the present
chapter has emphasized two: the recognition of observable causes and conditions of religious states,
and the important place that physical well-being occupies as a condition of religious well-being

CHAPTER III

A Study of Religious Dynamics

WHEN Henry Drummond was not yet through his student years he composed and read a paper in which he gave voice to the need of scientific spiritual diagnosis. He remarked that, instead of handling mankind in a lump, we ought to have definite means of judging the varying conditions and needs of the different individuals whom we try to help.[1] To illustrate by a single example the justice of Drummond's complaint, let us ask ourselves why it is that of two persons who have had the same bringing up, and who seek conversion with equal earnestness, one is ushered into the new life with shoutings and blowing of trumpets, as it were, while the other, however earnestly he may seek such experiences, never attains them at all. Even a superficial glance at the ordinary course of revivals will show that they are often far from accomplishing what is hoped from them. It is also evident that the hopes of receiving certain experiences, held out before "seekers," are frequently unfulfilled when the conditions are favorable. Among the cases that I have minutely analyzed there are 35 persons who have definitely sought for a striking religious transformation or conversion. Of

---

[1] G. A. Smith, *Life of Henry Drummond*, New York, 1898, 53ff.

these, 12 have been entirely disappointed, 5 partly but not utterly so, and only 18, or one half, have secured what they sought. I have found the same general results in an examination of scores of cases of seeking for the experience commonly called "entire sanctification."

Nor is this all. If we examine the present experience of a large number of mature Christians, we shall find relatively few striking variations; but if we ask for the early religious history of these same persons, we shall find the most remarkable diversities. In some cases childhood religion has grown mature without special agitation; in others there has been a definite conversion with volcanic outbursts of emotion; and between these extremes we shall find innumerable grades and varieties of disturbance, though with much the same outcome when adolescence is over.

Inadequate Theories.

These differences have never been satisfactorily accounted for, and indeed the question has hardly been raised except for the sake of hazarding a guess. "The explanation of sudden conversions," says Bain, "is no doubt to be sought in some overpowering impression upon the mind that supplies a new and energetic motive to the will, thereby initiating a new line of conduct. . . . Such changes occasionally happen, but not without terrific struggles which prove how hard it is to set up the volition of a day against the bent of years."[1] Here all sudden conversions are lumped together as though they were all of one type; all are declared to be accompanied by terrific struggles, and all are explained by a single circumstance.

Equally incomplete is the explanation of Nietsche when he snarls at Christianity because, as he thinks, it is not in contact with reality. He declares that Christianity cultivates "an imaginary psychology (nothing but self-misunderstandings, interpretations of pleasant or unpleasant general feelings, for example, the conditions of the *nervus sympathicus,* with the help of the sign-language of religio-moral idiosyncrasy—repentance, remorse of conscience, temptation by the devil, presence of God)."[2] Doubtless this statement contains some truth; yet it is as inadequate to explain the broad variety of experiences occurring under Christian influences as it is to explain the whole sphere of perception, normal and abnormal together.

Here and there a more probable hint has appeared. Thus, Havelock Ellis makes the remark that a sudden explosion of suppressed hypnotic centers is "the most important key to the psychology of conversion."[3] Leuba, speaking of the conversion of John Wesley, throws out this hint: "An interesting re-

---

[1] *Emotions and Will*, third ed., New York, 1876, 453f.

[2] *Antichrist*, Works, New York, 1896, xi, 253.

[3] *Man and Woman*, second ed., London, 1898, 292.

mark can be made here concerning the influence of
suggestion: it is as the change that God works in the
heart is being described that the very same transformation takes place in Wesley."[1] The same writer
also remarks that "the particular forms in which
affective states dress themselves are functions of the
intellectual atmosphere of the time."[2] This is undoubtedly a hopeful clew; but, when he goes on to
affirm that joy "is never altogether wanting, and is
always violent during the first hours or days that
follow,"[3] he misses an essential fact. Starbuck was,
I believe, the first writer to give adequate recognition, with empirical data, to the marvelous varieties
that cluster about such terms as conversion. He advanced a step toward their explanation, also, when
he showed that something more than a conscious
exercise of either intellect or will was central in adolescent conversions.[4] He came still closer to the
problem when he found imitation, example, etc.,
present as motives in fifteen per cent of his cases.[5]
Nevertheless, a moment's reflection upon the capacity of the average person to tell the truth regarding his own motives will reveal some insecurity in
these results and bring up the whole question of the
best method of getting at the facts. Another clew
emerged in Starbuck's admission that "much de-

[1] "Psychology of Religious Phenomena," *American Journal of Psychology,*
vii, 340.

[2] *Ibid.*, 357.   [3] *Ibid.*, 351.

[4] *American Journal of Psychology,* viii, 292.   [5] *Ibid.*, 281.

pends upon temperament."[1] Yet this clew has never
been followed up. In fact, this same writer, com-
menting on some of his cases, confesses that some
religious experiences "seem to come in the most un-
accountable ways."[2] Now, I venture to believe that,
if we could secure sufficiently full information as to
the conditions, every one of these cases would be seen
to conform to law.

The present study, accordingly, is an attempt at
a more complete analysis of individual cases than
has heretofore been attempted. If we can lay bare
the factors in a few cases that are fully accessible,
the information thus acquired may afterward be
of service in interpreting the broader differences of
sects and religions. To forestall misunderstandings, it may be well to state at this point that the
phrase "religious dynamics" is not intended to
convey, and cannot properly convey, any metaphysical meaning. The problem concerns the concomitance of certain groups of phenomena and nothing
more. The question of divine influences in the mind
of man and in history must stand in exactly the
same position at the end of such a study as it does
at the outset. Anyone who prefers to do so is at
liberty to interpret every result as a description of
the mode of God's working in the world. Nothing
in the study itself has any logical tendency to under-
mine this belief.

[1] *American Journal of Psychology*, ix, 110.   [2] *Ibid.*, 81.

Method of the Present Investigation.

Our task consists in looking for coordinations between specific inner states and tendencies and specific external circumstances. We are confronted at the outset with the problem of how to secure adequate data. In previous studies in the psychology of religion reliance has been placed upon the *questionnaire* method, which consists in securing from many persons written answers to printed questions regarding their experiences. This is doubtless a satisfactory method of securing certain facts, but our inquiry calls also for information which the writers of such papers ordinarily do not and cannot possess. Accordingly, my question list was so constructed and the answers so used as to make the latter not merely a record of certain facts, but also a reflection of the personality of the writer. These answers were also supplemented in various ways: First, personal interviews were had with a large proportion of the persons examined. The cross-questioning which these interviews made possible not only cleared up doubtful points in the papers, but also elicited many new and important facts. Second, a large proportion of the subjects were placed under careful scrutiny by myself and others, with a view to securing objective evidence as to temperament. These observations were guided by a carefully prepared scheme of temperamental manifestations. Third, interviews, based upon the same scheme, were had

8

with friends and acquaintances of certain of the persons under examination. Finally, in order to get at the facts of suggestibility, hypnotic experiments were made upon all the important cases that were accessible. Fuller description of some of these methods of gathering data will appear later.

The number of persons examined was 77. Of these, 52 were males and 25 females. Nearly all are college students who are healthy in both mind and body and have had the advantage of positive moral and religious training. Nearly all are just past, or are just passing out of, the adolescent period. The average age of the men was 24.8, and of the women (one case, 65 years of age, being excluded), 22. Though this narrows the range for the observation of temperament chiefly to the formative years, it brings these compensating advantages: the nearness of the chief religious experiences, the habit of introspective analysis specially characteristic of adolescence, and the naïve and spontaneous expression of personal facts. Again, a large majority of the subjects were brought up under the influence of the Methodist Church, which lays great stress upon personal religious experiences. The opportunity to study the effects of suggestion was therefore excellent. In general, in spite of some limitations of the field of observation, the differences in type of religious experience and type of mental organization were many and great. The accessibility of the material, moreover, and the opportunity to observe, ask questions, and experiment repeatedly—these easily outweigh all the limitations. It is, indeed, not easy to see how a more satisfactory set of cases could be secured.

Let us now turn to the variations in religious experience from individual to individual. The chief one, and the one with which this study is occupied, is in the degree of abruptness of religious changes. One person reaches a higher plane of the religious life by a process of development scarcely ruffled by excitement; another attains the same state by passing through a mental cataclysm. Some elements of the explanation lie on the surface. For instance, the striking changes occur chiefly among denominations that definitely aim to secure them. Furthermore, these denominations have discovered many of the conditions favorable for producing such changes, such as a particular type or particular types of preaching and appeal; the use of music, particularly of certain kinds; intense social feeling fostered by meetings; the provision of external acts, signs, or instruments—such as rising for prayers, or to indicate decision, going forward, the altar, the mourners' bench—all of which evoke expression of the inner state and thereby intensify it; and, finally, the fitting of all the conditions together so as to produce a climax or a series of climaxes. What we need to determine next is the mental mechanism to which all this appeals, and also the reason why it fails of its result in many cases in which the conditions give hope of success; for it is a matter of everyday knowledge in revival churches that of two persons brought up in the same manner, and apparently meeting the same conditions, one may experience a brilliant conversion while the other may experience no such states at all.

In order to secure definite ground for an hypothesis on this point, the persons under examination were divided into two groups: those who had experienced a marked transformation, and those who had not. The fact that religious changes show all degrees of rapidity and of emotional intensity made it necessary to draw this line with great care. In every case, therefore, which the papers left in doubt a personal interview was had. Striking transformation was defined as a profound change which, though not necessarily instantaneous, seems to the subject of it to be distinctly different from a process of growth, however rapid. As soon as the subject grasped this definition he was requested to classify himself, and his decision was accepted as final.

In the second place, a cross division was made on the basis of predisposition of the mind toward such experiences. Let us call this basis "expectation of transformation." A careful study was made of the home influences, the general Church environment, and the specific circumstances surrounding the religious awakening. Here, again, much had to be drawn out by personal interviews. A considerable number of the subjects were taught that one who has been religious from childhood does not need a marked conversion. Others indicated that their thoughts were never turned strongly in the direction of conversion. All such were classed as not expecting a transformation.

Combining these two modes of division, we secure two positive classes for minute study: those who expected a transformation and experienced one, and those who expected but failed to experience. In the working out of this scheme a third division was found necessary in order to tabulate cases in which these two classes overlap; for a number of persons who experienced a marked transformation were unsatisfied, and sought for something more without securing it, while others were satisfied but sought for a still higher experience in vain.

To do justice to the case it is necessary to note the caution that was exercised in making the classes. For example, in the class of those who expected but failed to experience there are included none who did not distinctly declare that they sought an experience without finding. Most, if not all, of them had subsequently learned how to be religious in spite of this disappointment, yet the struggle in a large proportion of the cases had been acute.

From theology the suggestion may come that possibly these persons did not really surrender themselves to God. But an *a priori* assertion, or rather guess, like this ought to have little weight as against the following: All the evidence of the facts goes to show that those who were disappointed had put themselves in the same attitude of will as the others; furthermore, a large majority of the disappointed ones are now living positively religious lives—in the evangelical sense of religious.

Temperament as a Factor in Striking Religious Transformations.

These two classes were next examined with respect to temperament. This was a laborious and perplexing undertaking, both on account of the unsatisfactory treatment of temperament by writers on psychology, and because of the complexity of the facts to be observed. It is easy for any psychologist to give a classification of temperaments that can be brilliantly illustrated from history, but it is quite another thing to devise a method for grouping the persons one comes in contact with. At the present day two classifications are employed. The first, represented by Wundt[1] and many followers, is based upon the fact that one's mental processes may vary in both rapidity and strength. This basis yields four temperaments which correspond fairly well with the traditional fourfold division. The rapid-strong tem-

---

[1] *Grundzüge der Physiologischen Psychologie*, Leipzig, 1893, ii, 519ff. See also Lotze, *Microsmus*, vol. ii, book vi, chap. ii; and Ladd, *Elements of Physiological Psychology*, New York, 1897, 572ff.

perament corresponds to the choleric, the rapid-weak to the sanguine, the slow-strong to the melancholic, and the slow-weak to the phlegmatic.[1] On the other hand, French writers for the most part adopt a qualitative basis, that is, classify according to the faculty or function that predominates. This is true of Ribot,[2] Queyrat,[3] Levy,[4] and Fouillée.[5] Perez, however, retains liveliness and intensity as the basis.[6] This is not the place to discuss the general topic of temperament, or to go into the merits and defects of these classifications. It is sufficient to remark that a practical scheme must provide at least a fairly definite mode of describing any and every person whose individuality is sufficiently marked to be noticeable.

Wundt's scheme was first employed, but it quickly proved itself inadequate to give a genuine characterization of many distinctly marked individualities. This was especially true when Wundt's classes were interpreted as if they were identical with the traditional four temperaments. The qualitative plan was next tried, but, while it supplemented the other, it proved inadequate taken by itself. In the interest of a workable scheme, therefore, it was found necessary to combine the two modes of division. The result was not a new classification of temperaments, but what

---

[1] For a brief description of the four temperaments, see pp. 206ff., 226f., 231f.

[2] *Psychology of the Emotions*, London, 1897, 388ff.

[3] *Les Caractères*, Paris, 1896, 36ff.

[4] *Psychologie du Caractère*, Paris, 1896, 182ff.

[5] *Tempérament et Caractère*, Paris, 1895, 20ff.

[6] *Le Caractère*, Paris, 1892.

we may call a scheme of the constituents of temperament. The mode of procedure now consisted first
of judging whether sensibility, intellect, or will was
the most prominent faculty; next, of finding the
second in prominence; then, of estimating the place
of each of the three faculties in respect to promptness
and intensity. For each subject, in the end, there
were three descriptive designations, as, for example,
prompt-intense intellect, prompt-weak sensibility,
prompt-weak will, and these three were arranged in
the order of prominence.

The sources of evidence for temperament were the
same as those employed by the writers just named,
namely, permanent modes of action, of speech, and
of point of view; permanent interests; likes and dislikes; habitual social interactions, etc., whether observed and recorded by the subject himself or by
other persons. The data were secured by the following methods: First, by inserting in the question
list mentioned in Chapter I, and reproduced in Appendix A, a number of questions concerning likes
and dislikes, laughter and weeping, anger and its
effects, habits of introspection, moods, promptness or
its opposite in decisions, ideals, the effects of excitement, habits with respect to physical activity, etc.
A particularly fruitful interrogation was the following: "If you were obliged to spend a whole day alone,
felt at perfect liberty to follow your inclinations, and
had the means to do so, what would you do?" At

no point in the questions was temperament or disposition mentioned.

The second method was by observation of the general tone of the papers. The question list, it may be remarked, was very lengthy. It included approximately two hundred specifications, all planned with reference to the evoking of memories rather than the securing of categorical replies. Its length precludes its presentation here. The responses were correspondingly extended, and not the least remarkable thing about them was the amount of information they imparted between the lines. It was obvious that they were not merely a record of phenomena, but also a body of original phenomena. Sometimes what they purported to be as a record had to be offset by what they were as new facts. Thus, in response to the question, "Do your friendships last?" nearly every writer gave an affirmative answer. Here it is probable that the ideal of the writers rather than their actual experience comes to expression. These answers have value, therefore, as evidence of the nature of the social instinct, but hardly as evidence of actually existing social relations. Occasionally the manner of responding to a question revealed more than did the content of the response. Intellectual interest stood out in one, strenuous seriousness or passionate earnestness in another, while the chattiness of a third revealed a type of impressionability strongly contrasted with both.

A third method was objective observation as already described. The scheme of questions underlying this part of the investigation was also extended.[1] It included among other topics the following: The habitual state of the muscles, particularly the face, whether tense or relaxed; one's carriage and motions, whether quick, jerky, irregular, or more slow, free, and pendulum-like; one's mode of speech and the quality of the voice; the expression of the eyes, and any other signs that show whether the subject is wide-awake to his surroundings; whether one is more given to the reception of impressions or to active effort to control surroundings; readiness to laugh and cry; specific manifestations of anger; characteristic moods; persistency; social self-assertiveness of various types; intellectual habits; religious habits.

The data obtained by all these methods were compared, and thus the final judgment was based upon a really wide range of facts. Furthermore, in most cases, independent judgments were formed by different observers, and these judgments were finally checked off against one another. As soon as a definite and comprehensive mode of procedure was discovered the facts began to fall into place with the sort of inevitableness that inspires confidence in one's method. The amount of agreement reached by observers independently of one another was another

1 See Appendix B.

evidence of the trustworthiness of the method. If the lack of precision and of quantitative determinations should seem to impair the value of the results, two considerations might be offered in defense. The first is that all the knowledge of temperament possessed by biographers and historians and by literary workers, and nearly all that possessed by psychologists themselves, has been gathered by methods analogous to this, though rarely, if ever, by methods so systematic and comprehensive. Dependence has not been placed upon any general or casual impression, but only upon large masses of data each item of which has been carefully scrutinized. The other consideration is that a manner of learning men similar to this, though far less comprehensive, is one of the bases of the world's successful business. Indeed, a large part of the practical interests of life hang upon our ability so to observe temperamental manifestations as to be able to predict the general quality of one's reactions in different sets of circumstances. Of course this is not a sphere in which claims to scientific infallibility become even plausible; nevertheless, the thorough and systematic analysis employed may fairly entitle the results to some degree of confidence.

The temperamental classification of the members of the three groups concerning whom adequate information was obtainable yields the following results:

RELATION OF STRIKING TRANSFORMATION TO TEMPERAMENT.

Classification According to the Three Faculties.	Sensibility Predominant.	Intellect Predominant.	Will Predominant.
GROUP I.—17 persons who expected a transformation and experienced it............	12	2	3
GROUP II.—12 who expected but did not experience	2	9	1
GROUP III.—5 others who belong to both the above classes......................	2	2	1

Classification According to the Four Temperaments.	Sanguine (Prompt-Weak).	Melancholic (Slow-Intense).	Choleric (Prompt-Intense).	Phlegmatic (Slow-Weak).
GROUP I.......	8	6	1	2
GROUP II......	2	3	7	

The most marked contrast in these tables concerns the relation of the two main groups to intellect and sensibility. Where expectation is satisfied, there sensibility is distinctly predominant; but where expectation is disappointed, there intellect is just as distinctly predominant. To appreciate the strength of this conclusion it will be well to remind ourselves once more of the range of facts upon which it is based. In only three cases in Group I and one case in Group II was it necessary to rely solely upon the subject's paper. A second interesting result is that those whose expectation is satisfied belong almost exclusively to the slow-intense and prompt-weak varieties, the temperaments approaching most nearly those traditionally known as the melancholic and sanguine. On the other hand, those whose expectation is disappointed belong more largely to the prompt-intense variety, or the choleric temperament, though the distribution between the choleric, melancholic, and sanguine is not markedly uneven. Again, comparing the two main groups with respect to promptness and intensity, each by itself, we find that, on the whole, Group II exceeds Group I in both promptness and intensity. Finally, some slight confirmation of the representative character of these results is found in the heterogeneity of the cases in Group III. The full significance of these results concerning temperament, however, will not appear until we have examined the same subjects with respect to automatisms and suggestibility.

×

Relation of These Experiences to Mental and Motor Automatisms.

Careful inquiry was made, both in the question list and by personal cross-questioning, for evidence of mental and motor automatisms. The inquiry divided itself into these heads: Striking dreams in connection with religious awakening; hallucinations in connection with religious transformation; hallucinations occurring at other times; motor automatisms occurring at the time of religious transformation, and similar automatisms occurring at other times. The purpose of the inquiry did not make it necessary to render these various classes rigorously precise. Accordingly, when it was difficult to decide whether a given phenomenon was to be classed as a dream or as an hallucination, I followed the impression of the subject. If he insisted that he was awake at the time, the experience was classed as an hallucination. Similarly, the group of motor automatisms contains some cases that fall near the boundary line; but, in general, it is believed that the list which follows is a full and substantially accurate census. It contains all the facts of these classes discovered in the entire investigation.

Striking Dreams in Connection with Religious Awakening.

Dreamed of being cast into hell. Suffered all torments of the damned that he had ever heard about.

Dreamed of being cast out of heaven.

Dreamed of a heavenly procession which he could not join.

Dreamed of taking an examination on fitness to go to heaven.

Hallucinations in Connection with Religious Transformation.

Streaks of light shone down.

A somewhat bright, diffused light just above the eyes. Occurred twice.

Seemed to observe the joy in heaven.

Saw a vision of the broad way and the narrow way, with many persons in the former and few in the latter.

Other Hallucinations.   •

Saw a light spring up from a tomb in a cemetery.

Used to hear his name spoken when he was about to commit some sin.

Had just retired after private devotion. Saw a dim, diffused light above the eyes.

Was touched by an absent friend.

Saw a dog that was not there.

Heard deceased grandfather's voice.

Heard mother's voice when she was far away.

Heard the voice of a friend.

Felt the presence of an absent friend. It seemed to be an objective fact and not a mere impression.

Heard music different from any he had ever listened to.

Heard angels sing.

In the midst of a public speech twice saw a scene he was describing.

Childhood fear of the dark has persisted. The feeling that a fiend is just behind and ready to spring upon him sometimes becomes so intense that self-control becomes impossible.

An inner voice which expresses approval at times of perplexity by saying, "Fear not, I am with you."

God tells her where things are that she is looking for. Also tells her things before they come to pass.

Voices and visions just before sleeping at night. Has often gone to the window or out of doors to see where the music came from.

Up to the age of thirteen used every night to see figures in the room.

When praying had a vision of an absent friend who gave just the information that was desired.

Waked one night and saw a great luminous eye in the ceiling. Thought it was God's eye.

Has repeatedly seen his deceased mother's face.

Saw a scene from his past life.

Saw Christ hanging on the cross.

Saw Christ transfigured.

Saw a vision of the judgment.

Motor Automatisms at the Time of Religious Transformation.

Uncontrollable laughter for fully five minutes.

A powerful thrill through the whole body.

Sudden clapping of hands before any change of feeling came.

Tobacco habit broken without effort or even seeking.

Other Motor Automatisms.

Automatic laughter.

At times something very holy seems to be dictating his thoughts.

Has always felt himself under two influences, one good and one bad, and neither of them any part of himself.

Surprising and incomprehensible outburst of defiance to God. Age, about ten or twelve years. Shook fist at the sky and told God he hated him.

"The Holy Spirit often fills me so that I feel light, and it's no trouble to walk and not feel tired." (A lady well advanced in years.)

Talking, singing, whistling to one's self. This seems, at times, to become an automatic, subconscious performance. A parent affected in the same way sometimes lets out secrets by this means.

Let us now ask how these phenomena, exclusive of the dreams, are distributed among the three groups. Of 18 persons in Group I,[1] 8 have had either hallucinations or motor automatisms. Of the 6 persons in Group III, 5 have had similar experiences. Hence, of 24 persons who have had a striking religious transformation 13 have also exhibited these automatic phenomena. But of the 12 persons (Group II) who sought a striking religious transformation in vain only one has had either an hallucination or a motor automatism.

The total number of persons examined with respect to automatisms was 77. Of these, 20 had exhibited such phenomena. Now, 13 of these 20 are found among the 24 persons in Groups I and III; that is, practically one sixth of the entire number of

---

[1] The variation in the size of the groups is due to the fact that in respect to some persons adequate information was obtainable on one point but not on another. It is for this reason that Group I contains 17 persons in one case, 19 in another, and 14 in a third. That is, there were 17 concerning whom it was possible to form a definite judgment with respect to temperament, 19 with respect to automatisms, and 14 with respect to suggestibility.

persons examined embraces two thirds of the cases of automatisms. Putting these results in the form of percentages, we get the following:

General average of automatisms for
77 persons .... 26 per cent.

Average for those who have experienced a striking religious transformation .... 54 "

Average for those who sought such a
transformation in vain......... 8 "

In other words, the average for those who had a striking religious transformation is twice as high as the general average, and nearly seven times as high as the average for those who sought such a transformation in vain.

If the general average of automatisms seems rather excessive, the following explanatory circumstances should be borne in mind: First, motor automatisms are included with hallucinations. Second, nearly all the persons examined are too young to have forgotten such experiences. Third, the cross-questioning already described brought out a number of facts not elicited by the *questionnaire* and not likely to be elicited by a census of hallucinations conducted by correspondence alone. Finally, it now becomes obvious that the high general average depends upon the presence of a relatively large number of persons who have experienced striking religious transformations.

The results here reached may be graphically represented by the accompanying squares. The shaded
portion of the first square indicates the general aver-

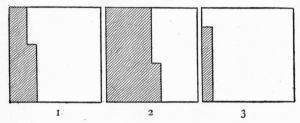

age of mental and motor automatisms. The shaded
portion of the second indicates the average for those
who experienced a striking religious transformation;
that of the third, the average for those who sought
such a transformation in vain.

These results are so unequivocal that interpretation is unnecessary. It may be worth while to add,
however, that in two cases of motor automatism occurring at the time of religious transformation there
was clear evidence of a congenital tendency to such
performances; in both cases a parent had exhibited
a similar automatism under similar religious conditions. In a third case it was possible to identify a
phenomenon as probably automatic through a similar
but more pronounced phenomenon in a parent. One
case of hallucination was likewise clearly referable
to congenital tendencies. Three of these four cases
of congenital proclivity belong in Group I. Furthermore, to Groups I and III belong nearly, if not quite,

all the persons who have experienced the healing of disease by faith, those who have received remarkable assurance of answered prayer in advance of the event, and those who reported other veridical premonitions. The conclusion is that the mechanism of striking religious transformations is the same as the mechanism of our automatic mental processes.

Suggestibility as a Factor in Striking Transformations.

There remains for study the relative suggestibility of the three groups; that is, their susceptibility to such influences as appear most strikingly in hypnotism. At first thought this seems to be a simple problem of more and less; but it is neither simple nor merely quantitative. Indeed, the qualitative varieties of suggestibility are quite as marked and quite as important as the "suggestibility and nonsuggestibility" which chiefly figure in the literature of suggestion. It must have struck many experimenters as a strange incident that, whereas persons of sound body and trained mind make excellent subjects, most of the literature represents suggestibility as identical with relative prominence of the lower centers. The fact seems to be that some persons are easily hypnotized, not because the higher rational centers are undeveloped, but precisely because the high development of these centers—the habit of prompt concentration of voluntary attention—makes it possible to follow the suggestions of the operator with precision. Moll remarks that the ability to direct one's thoughts in any particular direction is favorable to hypnosis, but that this ability is usually considered to be a sign of strength of will.[1] As the persons under examination in the present part of our study are, perhaps without exception, healthy, and as all have had considerable mental training, it will be seen that ready response to suggestion cannot be regarded as an unambiguous sign. The experimentation was begun under the tentative hypothesis that auto-suggestion might possibly account in part for the failure of persons in Group II to secure the desired experiences. The problem then became whether external suggestion was more prominent in Group I and auto-suggestion in Group II.

The problem may be more precisely put by distinguishing between passive suggestibility and spontaneous auto-suggestion. The necessity of thus stating the distinction grows out of the ease of misunderstanding certain phenomena, particularly those commonly described as "resisting the operator's suggestion." Thus, if a subject struggles to open his eyes when I tell him that he cannot do so, this is no evidence of spontaneity. For the very assertion, in the early stages of hypnosis, that the eyes cannot open is a challenge to try; it is a double suggestion. This was exquisitely demonstrated upon one of my

[1] *Hypnotism*, London, 1895, 40.

subjects. For some time I had tried in vain to close the eyes by making the usual passes and giving the usual suggestions of drowsiness, etc. At last the subject, who was apparently wide-awake, declared that she could not close them and keep them closed. Catching at this hint, I suddenly remarked, "You cannot close them!" They immediately clapped shut with every appearance of doing it automatically. In another case in which the usual suggestions seemed to have little or no effect the subject was instructed to keep his eyes closed voluntarily for a while. But his eyes opened very soon, and did so repeatedly. He finally declared that it seemed as if he *could not* keep them closed. In two other cases it was found that a previously formed conviction on the part of the subjects that they were suggestible had tended to make them appear more passive than they really were.

What was looked for, then, was evidence of spontaneity or originality rather than mere readiness of response or its opposite. An illustration or two will make this clear. To one subject I declared that his outstretched arm was rigid and could not move. The arm immediately stiffened out, but began a series of incipient up-and-down motions. This was clearly a product of my own suggestion, as were also, perhaps, the sympathetic writhings of the body and contortions of the face. The cataleptic arm was the right one. Presently the left arm was raised and began to push down on the right one, evidently in an effort to lower it. Failing in the effort, the left arm itself now became cataleptic, and could not lower itself. Here the evidence of spontaneous auto-suggestion is unmistakable. Contrast this, now, with another case in which a suggestion was given that an arm was cataleptic. Certain incipient responses to the challenge were made as before, but they ceased in a few seconds, while the face and the rest of the body expressed little or no interest in what was going on.

Let us compare two other cases that are less striking, and yet unambiguous. In both, passes in front of the eyes and suggestions of heavy eyelids, etc., meet with very slow response, so slow that I finally close the lids with my fingers. If, now, I say, "Your eyes are closed tight; you cannot open them," both subjects open their eyes. Similarly, they can unclasp their hands, and the like, whenever they are challenged to try. Thus far the two cases correspond point for point. But if, after closing the eyes, I leave the subjects alone, avoiding, as far as possible, the giving of further suggestions, a decided difference presently appears. One of the subjects sits with closed eyes for an indefinite length of time, that is, shows no initiative; but the other, as often as the experiment is repeated, spontaneously opens his eyes after a short interval.

Such experimentation resulted in separating the

cases according to two fairly well-marked types. In respect to readiness of response to hypnotic sugges- tion the two types do not seriously differ. Under both types fall cases in which the response was al- most immediate, and also cases in which it was very slow. But the behavior under suggestion was decid- edly different. Let us call the two types the pas- sive and the spontaneous. Under the former belong those who take no decided or original part in the experiment. Their response to external suggestion may not be very pronounced, but they initiate noth- ing after once they have begun to yield. Under the spontaneous type belong, on the other hand, the few who appear to be nonsuggestible and those who, while responding to suggestion, take a more or less original part by adding to the experiment or by waking themselves up.

Comparing Groups I, II, and III with respect to this point, we find certain plain differentiations. To begin with, as might be expected, nearly all the per- sons who have experienced any of the mental or motor automatisms already described are "passives." Thirteen such persons were experimented upon, and of these ten clearly belonged to the passive type. This fact makes it appear that the two types here de- scribed are substantially parallel with those sifted out by certain experiments at Harvard University.[1]

---

[1] *Cultivated Motor Automatism*, by Gertrude Stein, *Psychological Review*, v, 295ff.

A few cases were not accessible for purposes of experiment. The numbers experimented upon in the three groups were respectively 14, 12, and 5. The results are as follows: In general, the line between Groups I and II coincides with that between the passive and the spontaneous types, though apparent exceptions exist, and though the interpretation of the facts is not equally clear in all cases. Of the 14 cases in Group I (persons who expected a striking transformation and experienced it) 13 are of the passive type. Of the 12 persons in Group II (expectation disappointed) 9 clearly belong to the spontaneous type, 1 is entirely passive, and 2 are open to some doubt. Of the 5 persons in Group III (striking experience, yet disappointed) 2 are passive and 3 spontaneous. In the accompanying diagrams the shaded portions represent the percentage of passive suggestibility in each of the three groups:

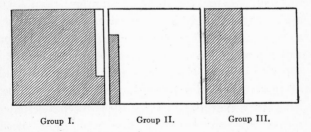

Group I.   Group II.   Group III.

The nature of the evidence may be further illustrated and the conclusion still further strengthened by reference to the negative and doubtful cases. The one case in Group I that is not clearly passive is the one first mentioned on a preceding page in illustration of the double character of many verbal suggestions. This case is therefore probably a passive one, though not so counted in the above figures. Another member of this group seemed for some time to be an exception to the general rule. She had had three striking experiences, and yet was apparently not suggestible. One day, however, mention having been made in the class in psychology of pain induced in a tooth by imagining a dental operation, she soon felt a toothache. It became intense and lasted for three or four hours, the face meantime becoming sore and apparently swollen. This settled the question of passive suggestibility. Turning, now, to the negative and doubtful cases in Group II, we find that the one clearly negative case is one that stands on the border between Groups I and II. This subject had more difficulty in classifying himself than any other one in either group. Again, of the two cases scheduled as doubtful, one is the only case in this entire group in which any form of mental or motor automatism was discovered. Nevertheless, the case remains ambiguous; for, though external suggestions are accepted with every sign of passivity, the subject has heretofore practiced auto-suggestion, even to the extent of curing toothache and other minor pains thereby. His present passivity, therefore, may be partly or wholly due to training. By way of parenthesis it may be remarked that each subject was questioned as to whether he had ever been hypnotized or had ever witnessed hypnotic experiments, and his reactions were judged according to his replies.

The correlation between one's religious experience and one's type of suggestibility was sometimes found to be curiously complete. Here, for example, is a subject whose response to passes and suggestions of drowsiness is not prompt; yet when the response comes it simply plumps itself. The subject is now very passive. In response to a suggestion an arm quickly becomes cataleptic. But, in the midst of the experiment, something having incidentally appealed to the subject's interest, he spontaneously opens his eyes and appears to be completely out of the hypnosis. This man was converted at the age of sixteen with marked manifestations. His whole being was thrilled with joy, and he had what he regarded as the witness of the Spirit. But from seventeen to nineteen he endured terrible storm and stress in which he sought in vain to recover his original status. He finally settled down to the conviction that we are children of God in our deeds and thoughts rather than in our particular moods and feelings.

A still more remarkable parallel is as follows: Response very prompt; lids clapped shut and trembled. At the suggestion that they could not open they quickly opened. The remark was then made that perhaps the lids would not close so promptly next time. The suggestion worked, for now it required many passes to shut the eyes. Arm refused to become cataleptic, but when I began to breathe deeply and slowly, as if asleep, the subject's head promptly began to fall over forward; it continued downward until it rested on the breast. Subject now apparently in a deep sleep; but after a while a spontaneous awakening occurs. He is now rehypnotized and told that he cannot pronounce his name; a gentle struggle ensues and lasts for a considerable time, but the effort is not given up until the name is successfully pronounced. The characteristics here are initial passivity followed after a while by decided spontaneity. This exactly describes the subject's religious experiences also. On two different occasions, after earnestly seeking for a marked experience, he happened to notice some incidental thing in his environment that he took to be a divine token. Immediately he experienced great exaltation. His heart's desire seemed to be realized. But after a few days the emotion waned, and reflection setting in pronounced a severe verdict upon the whole performance.

In order to appreciate the weight of these results concerning the relation of suggestibility to religious transformations, it will be necessary to notice once more the principle upon which cases were classed in Group II. This group contains no case in which there was not a distinct effort to obtain an experience that never came. Now, of the 77 persons examined there are many whose training and environment were equally adapted to induce expectation and seeking but did not do so. It is therefore probable that spontaneous auto-suggestion prevented expectation in some as it prevented the fulfillment of expectation in others. Hence, the sphere in which it plays a decisive rôle is undoubtedly much larger than the numerical proportions seem to indicate.

Moreover, no statistical display can do justice to facts of this sort. For not only must the numbers express in some degree one's interpretation of facts, and not merely the bare facts themselves, but the qualities with which we are dealing are too profound and pervasive to be expressed in any simple formula. The whole style of one's mental organization is involved. It is safe to say that any observer of human nature would perceive the propriety of setting off Groups I and II from each other on general grounds and without reference to the facts upon which this part of our study is based. The personalities in each group taken by itself are relatively alike, while the two groups are clearly different from each other. Psychology merely renders this obvious difference more precise by saying that the difference is one of temperament and of a more or less spontaneous attitude toward environment.

Three Favorable Factors in Combination.

It has been shown that three sets of factors favor the attainment of a striking religious transformation: the temperament factor, the factor of expectation, and the tendency to automatisms and passive suggestibility. Let us, in conclusion, note the effect of combining these three factors. Of 10 cases in which there is expectation of a marked transformation, together with predominance of sensibility and passive suggestibility, the number whose expectation was satisfied was 9. But of 11 cases of such expectation, together with predominance of intellect or of will, and with spontaneous auto-suggestion, not one was satisfied. These numbers include cases from Group III as well as from Groups I and II.

If our groups seem to contain rather few cases, it should be remembered that a problem of this kind requires relatively complete knowledge of a few cases rather than an item or two of knowledge regarding many cases. Our procedure must necessarily consist in a gradual narrowing down of the range of cases, together with increasing minuteness of scrutiny in each case. As a matter of fact, we have approached about as closely to the strict method of experiment as the subject permits. The factors are so definitely identified that prediction becomes safe wherever either of the two combinations just mentioned is found present. Given three factors, the fourth—the general character of one's religious experiences—can be predicted with a high degree of probability.

It is supposed by many that striking transformations in the affective life are reserved for those who have been great sinners. I know of more than one person who has been tempted to become a great sinner in order to be able to experience a brilliant conversion. The idea seems to be that an abrupt transition from moral badness to moral goodness naturally carries great emotional disturbances with it. And doubtless such circumstances do tend to intensify whatever happens. But it does not at all appear that these circumstances are the chief factors that determine the degree of affective transformation at conversion. For among the cases belonging to Groups I and III there is only a meager sprinkling of persons who had ever been bad in any very positive sense. In fact, of the entire 24 persons, only 5 report having experienced any sorrow for specific sins, and even then the sin repented of was generally a bad temper or some similar infirmity. On the other hand, of 13 persons in Group II, all of whom sought a striking transformation in vain, 3 also report sorrow for specific sins.

In short, everything goes to show that the chief mental qualities and states favorable to these striking experiences are expectation, abundance of feeling, and passive suggestibility with its tendency to hallucinations and other automatisms. Shall we therefore conclude that conversion is practically an automatic performance? Not unless we first define conversion so as to ignore its profound relation to God and to the principles of a good life. If conversion is a *moral* renewal, it is not mere psychical process of any sort. What has been proved is simply that, when conversion or an equivalent change takes place in one's moral attitude toward life and destiny and God, it may clothe itself in certain emotional habiliments provided certain factors are present, but otherwise not. The substance of religious experiences as far transcends their emotional forms as a man transcends the clothes he wears.

We may, however, draw from these facts a warning against mistaking the clothes for the man. "Would you cast the horoscope of a human life?" says Fouillée. "It is not to be read in the constellations of the sky, but in the actions and reactions of the interior astronomical system; do not study the conjunction of the stars, but those of the organs."[1] Similarly, we may now add: Would you understand the emotional aspects of religious experiences? Do not ascribe them to the inscrutable ways of God, but to ascertainable differences in men's mental constitutions; do not theorize about divine grace, but study the hidden workings of the human mind!

---

[1] *Tempérament et Caractère*, Paris, 1895, 88.

Explanation of Trances, Visions, the "Power," and the Like.

When the distinction just made has been firmly grasped we shall be ready to perceive, without being shocked by it, that the striking psychic manifestations which reach their climax among us in emotional revivals, camp meetings, and negro services have a direct relation to certain states of an essentially hypnotic and hallucinatory kind. In various forms such states have appeared and reappeared throughout the history of religion. Examples of what is here referred to are found in the sacred frenzy of the Bacchantes, the trance of the sibyls, the ecstasy of the Neo-Platonists, the enlightenment that came to Gautama Buddha under the sacred Bo-tree, the visions of the canonized saints, the absorption into God experienced by various mystics, and the religious epidemics of the Middle Ages, such as tarantism and St. Vitus's dance. All these and a multitude of similar phenomena were produced by processes easily recognized by any modern psychologist as automatic and suggestive. Similarly, the phenomenon in Methodist history known as the "power" was induced by hypnotic processes now well understood, though hidden until long after the days of the Wesleys. John Wesley was puzzled and troubled by these manifestations. For a time it was not uncommon for men and women to cry out in his meetings and fall unconscious, or seemingly so, to the ground. They appeared to be seized by some mysterious power that contorted their limbs or rendered their bodies rigid. They saw visions, heard voices, and became the organ of what seemed like revelations. Perhaps nothing in the career of Mr. Wesley more clearly reveals his marvelous practical capacity than his calm and, for the most part, common-sense treatment of such occurrences. A religious leader who had been in touch with ghost-experiences might be expected to be particularly impressed by these new phenomena. Nothing would seem more natural than that he should cultivate them, both as a means of attracting the attention of the masses and as an attestation of divine truth. This was, in fact, the policy of many religious leaders, as, for example, of Swedenborg. We have had some touches of that sort of religious propagandism even in our own country. Both Increase Mather and his son, Cotton, zealously asserted the truth of witchcraft because it seemed to prove the reality of spiritual things. But Wesley had the wisdom to perceive that these apparently divine or demoniac possessions were matters aside from his main business. As a result, though the "power" continued to accompany the Methodist movement for fully two generations, and has not even now entirely disappeared, it never in any way became grafted upon the stock of Methodist beliefs.

The explanation of the "power" and similar outbreaks is simple. Under the pressure of religious excitement there occurs a sporadic case of hallucination, or of motor automatism, or of auto-hypnotism taking the form of trance, visions, voices, or catalepsy. The on-lookers naturally conceive a more or less distressing fear lest the mysterious power attack their own persons. Fear acts as a suggestion, and the more suggestible soon realize their expectation. In accordance with the law of suggestion, every new case adds power to the real cause, and presently the conditions are ripe for an epidemic of such experiences.

Trances like that of the Buddha are brought about in substantially the same way, namely, by abstracting the mind from its ordinary multiplicity of interests and narrowing the attention until self-conscious control lapses and one seems to be absorbed in the infinite. The lapsing from one's self which is interpreted as the dissolution of individuality, or as absorption into divinity, can be easily experienced and understood through the practice of self-hypnotization. All that is necessary is prolonged fixation of attention upon any simple object. It is the process actually cultivated to-day by theosophists of the type of Mrs. Besant.

We should not be hasty in condemning all such states, for it is entirely conceivable that moral and religious ends are now and then really served by them. The divine Spirit might make a revelation to the Buddha or to some of the Hebrew prophets through a trance. About hypnotic processes as such there is nothing essentially bad or essentially good; everything depends upon their content and the use made of them. The modern mind, of course, does not look upon these phenomena as special evidence of the immediate presence of God or of a spirit; but no more should we regard whatever comes through this channel as necessarily worthless. The most that can be said is that, in general, the normal functions of the mind, or, if the expression be preferred, the functions that take place either instinctively or with the highest self-consciousness and self-control, are the ones most likely to bring forth a normal and healthful product. The ultimate test of religious values, however, is nothing psychological, nothing definable in terms of the *how it happens*, but something ethical, definable only in terms of the *what is attained* of loving trust toward God and brotherly kindness toward men.

Employment of Suggestion in Revival Meetings.

Thoughtful persons have again and again asked whether the persuasive power of a certain class of evangelists is not essentially hypnotic in character. For example, the pastor of a church in the State of Illinois related to me how an evangelist, by merely walking through the aisles of a church saying a word to persons here and there, and perhaps touching them, induced them to go forward to the mourners' bench in large numbers. But the pastor was puzzled by the fact that most of these persons were obviously unprepared to take such a step in real earnestness or with due appreciation of its significance. This was proved both by their lack of religious training and intelligence and by the utterly superficial results of the meeting. Within a few hours, if not minutes, a large proportion of those who were apparently penitent in the meeting were laughing the whole proceeding to scorn. The pastor was undoubtedly right in surmising that merely hypnotic or suggestive rather than moral or religious influences were the decisive ones in this case.

It is said that when a certain evangelist invited sinners forward he sometimes broke out, before a single person had started from his seat, into the exclamation, "See them coming! See them coming! See them coming!" meantime pointing to various parts of the crowded house. Now, if a professional hypnotizer should employ precisely the same means to bring subjects to the platform, he would probably succeed, though his power would go under some other name than preaching or oratory.

The law of suggestion is that one's ideas tend to realize themselves; that is, if anyone thinks of a state, mental or physical, he tends to fall into that state, and will do so unless this tendency is inhibited.

The thought of eating makes the mouth water; the thought of burglars in the house makes one hear them; listening to a singer who mismanages his voice has sometimes given musicians a sore throat. Suggestion works in proportion as it secures a monopoly of the attention. Let us ask what, according to this law, will happen to passively suggestible persons who submit themselves to certain well-known revival practices. Let us suppose that the notion of a striking transformation has been held before the subject's mind for days, weeks, or even years; let us suppose that the subject has finally been induced to go to the penitent form; here, we will suppose, prayers full of sympathy and emotional earnestness are offered for him, and that everything has been so arranged as to produce a climax in which he will finally believe that the connection between himself and God is now accomplished. The leader says to him, "Do you now believe? Then you are saved!" Is it not evident that this whole process favors the production of a profound emotional transformation directly through suggestion?

It does not necessarily follow that conversions thus brought about are worthless. The worth of the experience depends, not upon the presence or absence of suggestion, but upon whether it includes a decision and a renewal that reach deep into the springs of conduct. The form of John Wesley's conversion was perhaps determined by suggestion, but we know, from both his earlier and his later life, that his moral nature was now stirred to the depths. Suggestion, then, may lend shining garments to the change that takes place whenever the decisive determination of the will occurs; or, when the moral awakening is superficial, suggestion may delude into the belief that a given change is more profound than it really is. In the latter case we may look for evanescence like that of the morning dew. The danger, then, is that what is a product of mere suggestion should be mistaken for special evidence of the presence of God or of a renewal of character.

Another danger—greater, perhaps, than even this—is that the mind shall become expectantly fixed upon the attainment of some experience that the seeker's mental make-up will forever prevent him from attaining. Groups II and III are made up of persons who have suffered this misfortune. They were taught to seek something which their mental constitution renders practically impossible. And what was the result? In some cases square revolt against the entire notion of personal religious experience; in other cases an immense waste of nervous energy upon an impossible quest; in all cases those who were seeking to be God's children were made to feel like slaves instead of sons. One of them could not help feeling like a hypocrite whenever he took any part in church life because, in spite of his seeking, he had experienced none of the "so-

147

called religious experiences." He finally came to the conclusion that "there is nothing, absolutely nothing in religion (in the sense in which I take it the question is asked) that it seems to me I can absolutely rely upon." Another says of his conversion: "I was very happy that night, but the next day I was most wretched. It all seemed a mockery to me. . . . But I told no one my feelings, and was too proud to let anyone know how I had been deluded." He went on, however, trying to do all he could, and hoping that the experience would come some day, but it never came; he had to discover how to be religious in spite of this supposed lack. Still another writes: "I ushered myself into the faith that I would experience an overwhelming and constant joy, and peace unbroken and unexcitable; that I should have victory over a vicious temper, help in completely forgetting self and being at leisure from my own interests to help others, love for my enemies (so that they would eventually become my friends); and, finally, my idea of God's presence was peculiar, but I think common to many young converts—that there would be a strange inner purpose, a kind of tugging at my will power by a Power divine that would suggest to do and not to do. None of these things came out as I expected. I have ceased to believe that feeling has any religious significance. It seems to be subject to the most capricious moods."

The next instance that I desire to cite presents

features that are unusual but nevertheless instructive as showing what is to be expected from a certain type of revival work. "They told me," says the writer, "to read the Bible, and I read. They told me to pray, and I prayed. They said, 'Now, all you have to do to be saved is to go to the mourners' bench and ask God to forgive you, and be blessed.' They told me I would know the very instant that he saved me, and that I would know it just as definitely as I knew anything. I became greatly wrought up, and it was very hard for me to keep my seat when they called for those to rise who wished to be prayed for. I went forward night after night expecting a sudden reversal of my whole being. The meetings closed; I had had no change, no experience. I was the same afterward as I was before except that I was more or less disgusted and ashamed of myself to think that I had been so foolish. I almost concluded that it was all nonsense." During a subsequent season he tried again. "Here again," he says, "I expected a sudden change, but the change never came, and I was more than ever convinced that it was all bosh. I almost swore that I would never bother myself about it again, for I felt that I had given the matter due consideration." Still again he made the effort. "Often I arose from my knees almost mad at myself for praying after having prayed so often without results."

The cruelty unintentionally practiced upon those who desire to be disciples of Christ is, or ought to be, not a whit less revolting than the bodily mutilations prescribed by many a savage ritual. One among the persons responding to my *questionnaire* sought in vain for twelve years to attain what he was taught to expect; another sought for eight years, another for four or five. It clearly appears that many a consecrated soul endures a gnawing uncertainty and unrest concerning the favor of God. The papers show disappointment, confusion, a cloud upon the mind, reaction against the Church or even against Christianity itself. One writer came at one period of his career to conceive it as his highest ambition to prove to the world that it was possible to live a moral life irrespective of religion. That nearly all these persons finally found a more excellent way does not detract at all from the folly of the methods which brought them into suffering and antagonism. The facts cry out that we should apprehend more clearly what is essential and what incidental in religious experience.

The present study has necessarily been largely occupied with the consideration of religious incidents and abnormalities. In a subsequent one (Chapter V) the aim will be to offer a positive definition of what is essential and normal in spiritual life.

CHAPTER IV

A Study of Divine Healing

THAT religion has some relation to health is clear from almost every page of the history of religions. It is manifest, likewise, in contemporary religious phenomena. We need not go back to the time when as yet the distinction and consequent division of labor between religion and theology on the one side and the sciences and arts on the other were unknown —when the medicine man was at once healer, miracle worker, wise man, and revealer of the will of the divinities; for our own most enlightened communities furnish examples of considerable groups of men and women to whom religion itself means health of body as well as of soul. Nay, there are those among us to whom the indwelling of the divine Being seems to imply such inspiration and power of execution as practically to dispense with laborious study in the acquisition of the fine arts, at least the art of music. Even within the two great branches of historical Christianity, the Catholic and the Protestant, there lives and even flourishes a belief in the efficacy of faith, of relics, or of the intercession of saints.

Every one of these groups, too—Christian Scientists, faith healers, and adorers of relics—is ready to have its belief judged by the fruits of it in the actual

restoration of the sick to health. If there ever was
a day when the evidence thus offered could properly
be put aside with a sneer at human credulity, that day
has gone. These things are not done in a corner.
On every hand we are invited to come and see; and
any disposition that may be shown to ignore the facts
thus open to observation, while at the same time
wholly condemning the beliefs in the name of which
they are wrought, justly leads to a charge of prejudice and lack of scientific method. In fact, the evidence of most remarkable cases of healing under all
these systems of belief is so abundant that I shall not
hesitate to assume without argument that we are here
dealing with one or more genuine curative agencies.

For the sake of completeness certain other groups
of beliefs and apparent facts, though antagonistic to
those already mentioned, may be classified with them.
Witchcraft, for example, presents in its malignant
influence upon health the exact counterpart of the
systems of healing already referred to. The theory
is that, by means of powers and influences loaned by
the prince of darkness, the witch or wizard is able to
practice upon the health and even life of men without recourse to any means recognized by human
science. Thus, a witch can torment a victim by
merely fixing her evil eye upon him, or by sticking
pins into a figure made to represent him. Witchcraft, in fact, is never more than half understood
until we recognize in it a mediæval doctrine amount-

ing almost to a belief in both a good and an evil divinity. The kingdom of Satan corresponds with the kingdom of God. Thus, Satan has his priests, his solemn assemblies, his sacraments, his vows, his ministering angels, all corresponding point for point with the Christian belief of the time. Just so, the control over nature exercised by Christ and the apostles and granted to men of faith has its counterpart in black magic. To deny without examining the evidence that diseases were actually produced by these supposedly demoniacal influences would be on the same level as the parallel denial of the cures claimed in our own day in the name of religion. Indeed, it is scarcely credible that there should be no fire where there was so much smoke. The very fact that witchcraft was implicitly believed by the whole of Europe for many generations carries with it a strong probability that it had some basis in fact, however inadequate and misunderstood. Between these extremes, witchcraft on the one side and divine healing on the other, lie many groups of apparently related phenomena, such as healing under the inspiration or guidance of spirits, or by "animal magnetism," mesmerism, or the mind cure with its various names. Finally, the medical profession of the present day makes large use of modes of healing that dispense, in certain classes of cases, with the use of drugs or other physical means, and substitute therefor processes recognized as wholly mental.

All these modes of producing or removing disease have so thorough a *prima facie* resemblance that we may be reasonably confident of actual community between them in some underlying law of nature. To show the existence of such a law and its applicability to certain religious problems of our day is the main purpose of the present study.

A Bit of History.

In spite of the intrinsic importance and the striking character of the facts or alleged facts just referred to, and in spite of much apparently good evidence for them, not until the present generation were they made an object of anything like thorough scientific study. The reasons for the omission are not far to seek: they lie in all the influences that caused the scientific study of matter to precede the scientific study of mind, and in the apparently inextricable mingling of superstition, delusion, and fact. Even yet there are many men of science who have such a horror of defilement by contact with superstition that they are scarcely willing to approve the scientific exploration of that swamp land of the human mind, spiritism and its affinities. In the interest of the purity of science the most obvious course to pursue with regard to these apparently preternatural cases of healing and the reverse was to label them all "superstition" or "delusion" and cast them all on the rubbish heap of science. But the portentous mass of testimony could not be permanently disposed of by a scoff. And so it came about that, in spite of sneers and danger of losing scientific standing, various students dared to treat the facts as a subject for serious inquiry.

Mesmer's performances at the close of the last century gave the initial impulse to such studies. Nevertheless, up to a few years ago investigation was spasmodic and for the most part unfruitful. A shining exception is the work of the Englishman Braid, at about the middle of this century. His researches had actually led to the introduction of hypnosis as an anæsthetic agent in surgery, when this really great discovery was overshadowed and forgotten through the apparently still greater discovery of the surgical uses of ether and chloroform. Thus it came about that mental healing did not attain standing as a scientific fact until the present generation.

The new movement may be dated from the publication of either one of several works, such as D. H. Tuke's *Illustrations of the Influence of the Mind upon the Body,* the first edition of which dates back to 1872, or Bernheim's *De la Suggestion,* which appeared in 1884. The latter, which in the English translation bears the title *Suggestive Therapeutics,* stands related to scientific mental healing much as Darwin's *Origin of Species* does to the theory of evolution. At the present time, though gaps remain in our knowledge, much that was once doubtful has been verified, much that was mysterious has been reduced to law, and a multitude of investigators is pressing closer and closer upon the secrets that remain. The fact of mental healing is fully recognized, its general law has been formulated, and in many hospitals and in the private practice of many physicians this law is being practically and systematically applied for the removal of many disorders.

The Law of Mental Healing Stated and Illustrated.

The law, which is called the law of suggestion, can best be approached by analyzing a few of our most homely experiences. To begin a long way from the center, everybody knows that emotion has profound effects upon the body. It makes us weak, as in fear, or weary, as in anxiety or even from excess of joy. Emotion affects the appetite, the circulation of the blood, and the functions of nutrition and secretion. Some emotions are distinctly healthful, and others, when much indulged, are as distinctly unwholesome. A cheerful state of mind tends to good digestion and to a good general tone of the system. This is the reason why table talk, as is everywhere recognized, ought to be of a light and pleasant kind. The maxim, "Laugh and grow fat," is kept alive by its inherent truth. Again, not only is it true that indigestion tends to give one the blues, but also, conversely, that the blues tend to give one indigestion.

Of all the emotions, however, perhaps fear has the most serious ill effects. "There is no more effectual depressant, no surer harbinger of disease than fear," says Tuckey. "Much of the immunity from infection enjoyed by physicians and nurses is due, partly to the preoccupation of their minds, which leaves no room for selfish terror, and partly to the confidence begotten by long familiarity with danger."[1] Emotion, then, has much to do with health and disease, and mental healing will, accordingly, be found to consist, in no small degree, in replacing depressing states with more cheery and invigorating ones.

It is a matter of common knowledge that many physicians, either through natural endowment of disposition, through their unconscious manners, or through a deliberately cultivated art, have a wholesome influence upon their patients entirely apart from any physical treatment that may be administered. In fact, no physician can avoid administering much more than his medicines, whether that something be helpful or deleterious. Under precisely this principle the various forms of divine healing have an initial advantage, in that they point the mind of the patient to an infinite supply of beneficent power. Thereby fear is allayed, hope is begotten, and the atmosphere of the mind becomes salubrious.

Thus far we have considered nothing but the emotional state, which may be compared to the mental

---

[1] C. Lloyd Tuckey, *Psycho-Therapeutics*, London, 1891, 14.

atmosphere. Let us next note the physical effects of specific ideas. These may be compared to the objects that are seen through the atmosphere. Let the mind dwell for a moment, let us say, upon the look of peaches and cream standing upon the table and all ready to be eaten. The result is that the mouth waters. Let us analyze this everyday occurrence. The ideas were those of food and eating, and by merely holding them in the mind we found certain of the organs employed in eating aroused to their normal function. There was no intention of setting the salivary glands at work, but they proceeded as if the food thought about had been actually placed in the mouth. There appears to be a real connection, therefore, between the physical function and the idea of it, or of something habitually associated therewith.

It would be easy to show the same thing with various other physical functions. Who does not know, for instance, that the fear or even thought of blushing is often enough to suffuse the cheeks? Ask a sensitive person why he is blushing, and he will blush for response. By a faithful application of this principle orators and actors can at last train themselves to shed real tears upon demand. Nausea may be induced by the mere recollection of a previous nauseating experience. A bit of tainted food takes away the appetite for all food. The feeling of sea-sickness may be revived by merely stepping aboard an ocean steamer and smelling the odors from the galley and the rubber mats. A person who had suffered from seasickness within sight of a certain piece of shore could not look upon a photograph of that part of the coast for weeks thereafter without suffering a partial return of the original misery. The heart is decidedly subject to similar influences, as when the pulse becomes rapid from the thought that it is to be examined. A physician informs me that it is common for the pulse of healthy applicants for life insurance to become abnormally rapid, and even to necessitate the postponement of the examination, all because the thoughts are turned in the direction of the heart.

Functional performances, normal and abnormal, may often be suppressed in the same way. Hence, patients in a sanatorium are likely to be advised not to converse with one another about their complaints. To get one's mind into the right channel physicians frequently advise "a change of scene." Now, change of scene is often nothing more or less than a method of mental healing. Again, one can sometimes postpone or even stop a tendency to cough by resolutely thinking about something else, whereas thinking about it is one of the surest means of prolonging it. Similarly, when laughter becomes self-conscious it goes on of itself and may eventually become uncontrollable. I once made an impromptu experiment upon inhibition by suggestion. To a person who was on the point of sneezing I suddenly exclaimed,

"You cannot sneeze!" To the amazement of the person experimented upon, the incipient sneeze was instantly inhibited so that it never executed itself.

A child stubs its toe and falls. Immediately it looks up to its mother with surprise and doubt plainly engraved upon its features. It has every appearance of looking for its cue. If the mother shows alarm, and offers to sympathize with the supposed pain of the child, the latter bursts out into agonized weeping. But if the mother smiles, and assumes that the fall has done no harm, the child takes that cue with almost equal readiness. A boy of perhaps eight or nine years was troubled with a slight asthma. Whenever he returned from a visit to his grandmother he was audibly worse. The mother said that it came about in this way: The grandmother would say, "Come here, child, and let me hear you breathe!" Then followed exclamations and fussing and coddling until the child believed that he was in a bad way, and actually returned home with his asthma perceptibly aggravated.

Apparently, suggestion might carry very susceptible persons into their grave. There may be truth in the story—it has respectable authority for itself —that a French prisoner actually died from the belief that he was being bled to death. Experimenters pretended to open an artery in one of his arms, concealing the arm meanwhile from his view. To simulate the flowing of blood, they caused a stream of

warm water to trickle upon the supposed wound.
The prisoner, believing that he was bleeding to death,
is said to have gone through all the appropriate
symptoms, and finally to have died as the result of
the experiment.

Let us now formulate the law that is indicated in
these examples. It is that the thought of a function
tends to bring on that function, and the thought of
its contrary tends to inhibit it. More briefly expressed, the bodily life tends to conform itself to our
ideas of it. The suggestion may be direct or indirect;
that is, a function may be brought on by thinking
of the organ itself in a certain way, or by thinking
of some circumstance in which the organ might be
placed. The salivary glands might be set at work
by merely thinking how watering of the mouth feels,
or by looking at peaches or other food with no distinct thought of the mouth. In both cases the law of
suggestion finds exemplification.

From these simple illustrations of suggestion in
everyday life we pass on to experiment proper.
A simple experiment, first performed by Braid, consists in having a person fix his eyes and his attention
for several minutes upon any point in the palm of
his hand. This is generally enough to produce a
distinct sensation at the point of regard. The experiment may be varied, however, and rendered
somewhat more certain of results, by telling what sen-
sations may be looked for, such as cooling, burning,

tickling, tingling, pricking, numbness, aching. I have performed the experiment many times, and with unvarying success. On one occasion I remarked to a medical gentleman who was the subject of the experiment that sometimes the effects did not disappear for as much as two hours. Upon meeting him a few days later he informed me that some two hours after the experiment he found himself actually rubbing the palm of the hand that had been experimented upon.

In respect to this and all the other experiments about to be referred to we approach ground that may become dangerous to some persons. It is already evident that suggestion is an instrument of great and subtle power, and not one to be handled unwarily. In a subsequent section these dangers and the needful precautions will receive specific discussion.

The fact brought out in the experiment just described was known more than a century ago by a celebrated lecturer on surgery by the name of Hunter. "I am confident," he said, "that I can fix my attention to any part until I have a sensation in that part."[1] Johannes Müller, a great physiologist of the second quarter of this century, said nearly the same thing in another way. "It may be stated as a general fact," he observes, "that any state of the body which is conceived to be approaching, and which is expected with certain confidence and certainty of its

---

[1] Quoted by Tuke, 35f.

occurrence, will be very prone to ensue, as the mere result of the idea, if it do not lie beyond the bounds of possibility."[1] Strange that these really startling propositions from high medical authority did not force the medical profession to see that a new curative law lay ready for discovery.

It is easy enough to verify to some extent what Hunter and Müller claimed. Almost anyone with a trained mind who will persevere in the experiment will be able to do all that Hunter described. I have practiced upon myself, as far as was consistent with the avoidance of all danger of harmful interference with the natural functions, with unqualified success. In the parts of the body that have received the most training in this direction a suggestion of warmth, of tingling, or of pain receives most ready response. In the hands, arms, and lower extremities I can produce a distinct sensation almost instantly.

We shall presently see that the production of pain by suggestion is probably more easy than the removal of it. But that various aches and pains can be thus banished is also easy of experimental demonstration. Tuke relates an amusing instance of his own experimentation. He was about to have a tooth extracted under the influence of laughing gas when, through an accident to the apparatus, it became impossible to administer the gas. "The extraction was therefore performed without it," says Tuke, "but the

[1] Tuke, 36f.

163

operation was rendered almost painless by the writer
vividly imagining pleasant ideas, and mentally repeating to himself, 'How delightful! how delightful!' "[1] I have myself repeated this experiment, or
what amounts to substantially the same thing, during the filling of sensitive teeth, and with the same
results. A pupil of mine has succeeded in going
through a similar operation entirely without pain.

Relation of Mental Healing to Hypnotism.

The point at which our discussion has arrived
gives us an outlook upon a number of intensely interesting and highly important problems. As yet, it
will be noticed, only the most rudimentary applications of the law of suggestion have been touched
upon. We must ultimately go on to inquire into the
modes and extent of its application as a therapeutic
agent, and into its bearing upon divine healing and
similar phenomena. At present let us consider briefly its relation to hypnotism. Thus far the discussion has purposely avoided mentioning this topic,
because what needs to be made plain at the outset is
the essential identity in principle between mental
healing and many of our most commonplace experiences. There is, in fact, nothing occult or even rare
in the fundamental law involved. Even if we knew
nothing about hypnotism we should still have enough
accessible facts to warrant a safe induction as to how

[1] P. 58.

mental healing and similar processes succeed. Nevertheless, it is undeniable that the study of hypnotism has been the chief source of our scientific knowledge on this point.

It is essential that we make clear to ourselves that, while suggestion and hypnosis are not the same, the law of suggestion is, as far as science can now see, the fundamental psychological law employed in all hypnotic processes. The actions of a hypnotized person, then, are to be understood psychologically by reference to the very same law which we found exemplified in the watering of the mouth when one thinks of food. There is enough of mystery about even this latter event, but the mystery is not different from that which surrounds the whole subject of the hypnotic trance. The superstitious fear with which many persons look upon this state is no more reasonable than would be a similar dread of electric lights and electric cars. One is no more uncanny than the other, for both follow definite laws which, in spite of some remaining mystery, have been made out with sufficient fullness to give us control of the facts. It is, to be sure, dangerous to trifle with either hypnotism or electricity. Neither should be handled except by persons specially trained and instructed therefor. Nevertheless, in the case of both hypnotism and electricity, we carry the explanation back to the most commonplace events of our everyday life.

Since the state of hypnosis involves merely one

specific application of the law of suggestion, it would be an error to say that all mental healing is by means of hypnotism. When Christian Scientists and faith healers deny that their cures are wrought by hypnotism they do not deny that such cures are wrought by suggestion. Suggestion is, indeed, an omnipresent and all-pervasive agency, most subtle in its ways of working, and productive of effects of many different grades. Its ill effects range from the mere uneasiness occasioned by a thought of possible harm to, perhaps, death itself. Its good effects, on the other hand, reach all the way from the physical benefit of a momentary hope to restoration to health from some most distressing complaints.

For our present purpose the essential fact about the hypnotic state is that it involves what we may call a focusing of suggestion. The operator secures control of his subject largely by an artificial reduction in the number and insistence of competing ideas. This principle may be illustrated without resorting to hypnosis at all. Thus, every rider of a bicycle knows how hard it is, when one is learning to ride, to steer clear of obstacles, even under the most favorable circumstances. This remains true, also, for some time after one has learned to balance and guide one's machine. Something apart from one's self seems to take possession of the muscles or of the wheel. The explanation is that the thought of running into the post or the stone that one sees ahead is so vividly present to the mind as to control the muscles even against the will. The experienced rider avoids such obstacles not by thinking about them more intensely, but just the reverse—by scarcely thinking about them at all. Now, I have discovered in myself, and confirmed the discovery by questioning scores of riders, that it is easier to ride through some difficult places in the dark than it is by daylight. One rider, traversing a certain road for the first time by night, rode through a long, very narrow, and dangerous path unconscious of peril—a path which he says he could not use again after daylight revealed its true nature. Again, sandy patches of road which compel a rider to dismount during daylight have been passed over without serious embarrassment in the dark. In this case the difficulty was known, but, being less obvious to the senses, it had less paralyzing effect upon the muscles; in other words, the competition of ideas was reduced, and so the idea of going ahead was able to have more than usual effect. Thus we see how much more there is in even our everyday actions than deliberate volition.

This is the principle of which the hypnotist takes advantage. He narrows the attention of the subject to one or a few ideas, and thus secures a maximum effect from them. It is, furthermore, a law of the mind that any image that secures exclusive possession of the mind is regarded as a reality. This is one reason why our dreams are so real to us while

they last; they have few competitors or none. Just
so, a hypnotic subject may be made to feel cold or
hot by being told that he does feel so; he may seem
to himself actually to hear, see, touch, what he is told
is thus present to his senses. Let the operator tell
him that he has a headache, and a real ache sets in;
and when the operator declares that the ache is gone,
behold! so it is.

If, now, as we have abundantly illustrated, the
thought of any bodily function tends to produce that
function, what may we not expect when the attention, as in the hypnotic state (at least the deeper
states), becomes wholly concentrated upon a single
function or group of allied functions? Many apparently magical or miraculous results have thus
been attained. Needles have been run into the flesh
without hurting; surgical operations have been performed without the knowledge of the patient;
wounds have been healed with almost incredible
rapidity, and childbirth has been rendered practically painless. These extreme cases are, of course,
rare, for suggestibility has many degrees in different
persons. But the occurrence of these and many other
marvels is thoroughly authenticated.

Results of the same general nature, though less
in degree and narrower in range, can be wrought
upon anyone who can be hypnotized, and generally
in proportion to the depth of the hypnosis in other
respects. Probably ninety per cent of the population,

exclusive of infants, imbeciles, and the insane, can, under favorable conditions, be hypnotized. Furthermore, many of the effects of hypnotic medical treatment can also be produced entirely without hypnotization. A striking example of this will be cited farther on. Bernheim, indeed, has succeeded in producing practically all the simple characteristic effects of hypnosis, one by one, without hypnotizing at all.[1]

One may practice hypnotic suggestion upon one's self. Tuckey says: "Liebeault [from whom Bernheim derived his method of hypnotizing] tells me that he is able to cure himself of slight maladies—such as facial neuralgia—by auto-hypnotism and auto-suggestion. He sends himself to sleep by fixing his gaze upon some prominent object, such as a door handle, and his mind on the disappearance of the malady, and he drops off into a doze, out of which he awakes cured."[2] This is a perfectly simple and easy process for persons who have trained their minds to this kind of concentration. Perhaps at this place it ought to be remarked that the experience of myself and my pupil in the dentist's chair, which was referred to a little way back, included a definite process of self-hypnotizing.

A Word of Warning.

It is now high time to remind ourselves that what is harmless or even beneficial when properly handled

---

[1] *Suggestive Therapeutics.*   [2] *Psycho-Therapeutics,* 17.

may become deleterious in the absence of knowledge and skill. Since suggestion is all-pervasive in our lives it is proper that the public should understand its principles and how to take advantage of them. But this is not the same as advising indiscriminate experimentation. Indeed, the very fact that idea and function are so intimately and complexly inter-woven should teach us that, except within the sphere of the commonplace, the practical handling of sug-gestion should be left to experts.

This general consideration is supplemented by several specific facts. The first is that, while the organism is easily thrown out of order by suggestion, it is not so easily restored to its normal condition. The reason is that a sensation produced by sugges-tion, particularly if it is a painful one, acts as an added and independent suggestion, and so tends to counteract those of a contrary sort. Pain tends to keep itself going, that is, by merely calling our at-tention to itself. In addition, the remnant of super-stition almost always lurking in the mind makes amateur experimenters peculiarly easy victims of fear whenever anything goes wrong. It would be easy, for example, to get into trouble over so simple an experiment as that of gazing at the palm of the hand in order to produce a sensation; for various pains or numbness might result which would be suf-ficiently obstinate to give genuine discomfort and to defeat for an indefinite time all efforts to remove them. The positive danger of performing any similar amateur experiments upon the vital organs is obvious enough.

Again, it must never be forgotten that an indispensable part of every safe method of treating disease is competent diagnosis. No one is competent, in general, to practice any healing art who is not prepared to understand the nature of the complaints for which he prescribes. This is so nearly self-evident with respect to the more serious complaints which are usually committed to the care of physicians as to need no discussion. But even what seem to be insignificant complaints may, in reality, be symptoms of some serious disorder. A physician points out that so slight a symptom as a headache may be a warning of something that calls for the highest medical skill, so that to attempt to stop it by suggestion, or even to succeed in doing so, may give the larger opportunity for the progress of the disease.[1]

Furthermore, as will appear more fully later on, the medical profession, and particularly the specialists in nervous diseases, are fast adopting and putting into skillful practice the principle of suggestion. Their long study, their slowly acquired skill, are at the service of any patient who needs that kind of treatment. And who except a scientifically trained

---

[1] A. H. Burr, " Why Suggestive Therapeutics Should Not Be Taught to the Laity," in *Suggestive Therapeutics* (Mag.), November, 1898.

physician should be trusted to decide what kind of treatment each difficulty calls for? In a word, suggestive therapeutics is on the same plane as any other medical discovery. Properly employed, it is of inestimable service, but in the hands of ignorance it may produce the most harmful consequences.

What, then, is left to the discretion of those untrained in medical science? For it is plain that we cannot avoid employing suggestion to our weal or to our woe every day that we live. A few applications of its principles are perfectly feasible. For example, we can deliberately cultivate cheerful states of feeling, and we can assist others to be happy. If all the world should adopt such a course of living, the occupation of the doctors would be cut in two inside of ten years. Again, just as any intelligent layman is competent to make a proper use of some of the commoner drugs, as, for instance, in the case of minor cuts, burns, and bruises, so, it may be contended, specific suggestion for specific ailments may be allowed when the nature of the ailment is understood. To take the simplest case, what possible objection could there be to one's overcoming an attack of sleeplessness by suggestion? Again, if one has certain knowledge that a given headache has been induced by temporary and trivial causes, no harm could easily result from treating it after the manner of Liebeault. In general, too, the pains we have to bear, even under the care of the highest medical skill, can often be lessened by a proper direction of the attention. Here belong the chronic difficulties that have been already diagnosed and treated by the family physician. In short, just as wise dieting, proper clothing, and much more has to be attended to by ourselves, so there is a general and very necessary household use of suggestion as an adjunct of ordinary medical practice.

Misleading Sensations.

Let us now return to the main highway of our discussion. We have endeavored to disentangle and bring to clear view the great law of mental suggestion, exhibiting it both as an omnipresent fact in all our waking hours, and as a specialized fact in hypnotism. We have seen that it is sufficient to account for a great deal in the way of bodily healing. It is now necessary to remark that what seems to be healing is often no such thing at all, and that, furthermore, the visions and other apparently objective experiences that sometimes accompany divine healing have their explanation also in the law of suggestion.

We have seen how suggestion produces hallucinations in hypnotized persons, but we do not need to resort to hypnotism in order to witness these phenomena. For, just as the idea of a motion tends to bring that motion to pass, so the idea of a sensation tends to produce the sensation itself. For example, something makes us guess that the room is too warm or not warm enough, and presently we are perspiring with the heat or shivering with the cold, while all the time the temperature is normal. We are liable to taste in our food what we expect to taste; and sometimes an unpleasant taste that is too weak to be noticed of itself becomes unbearably strong as soon as our attention is called to it. When anyone points his fingers at your ribs, do you not have the very sensation of being tickled? How easy is it, when one is alone in a building at night, to hear whatever one's fears may suggest! Thus the thought of a sensation either intensifies one already present or even evokes one for which there is no discoverable external stimulus.

The following story came directly to me from one who remembered the time when stoves first came into general use. When it was proposed to warm churches by this means considerable opposition was made on the ground that stoves would render the air too close to be fit for breathing. One sister declared that she knew she should faint away the first Sunday her church was heated in that manner. The stove went in, however, and, sure enough, on the first Sunday thereafter, the good sister was carried out of meeting in a faint. But, on that day, the stove and its connections not having been completed, the church was as fireless as it ever had been.

How far, indeed, sensation can be controlled by

suggestion would hardly be guessed by anyone not already familiar with the experimental production of illusions and hallucinations. In the psychological laboratories it is found necessary to guard with the utmost diligence against the influence of suggestion upon observations and measurements of sensation. Experiments have also been devised to show how even our commonest estimates of size, weight, direction, etc., are fairly infested with inaccuracies arising from this source. Furthermore, it is possible not merely to over or under estimate or misinterpret, but also to manufacture a whole new sensation. By persisting in the right sort of training, one can bring one's self to the point of seeing what is not there at all. There is no trick about it, either; all that is necessary is to fix and concentrate the attention upon the idea of the desired sensation. For several years it has been my custom to illustrate this law of hallucination before my class in psychology by actually producing hallucinations in its members. Without my attempting any deception or concealment whatever, as high as twenty-five per cent of a large class has been made to see objects not present in the room at the time. Hypnosis was not at all resorted to, nor was there any failure to discriminate between a mere memory image and an actual sensation.

Under this principle it comes about again and again that the patient of Christian Science or of faith-healing practice, or of allied modes of treatment, imagines himself to be cured when nothing of the sort has happened. I have seen a faith healer work up great enthusiasm in cripples and persons partly blind by insistently suggesting that they were better. Glasses, ankle braces, and crutches abandoned—this proves nothing definite. We need to know how often—and it is not seldom—these helps have to be resumed. Furthermore, we must take into account the fact that the way is not open for a public avowal of failure to heal as it is for such avowal of success. Indeed, even if the managers were willing to present any trustworthy statistics, the victims would be restrained from testifying by their pride, their mortification, or even by their hope that they may yet be cured in spite of a first failure.

Thus, not only is the law of suggestion sufficient to account for much at least of the success of the modes of healing here under consideration, but it is likewise fitted to be a source of exaggerated and in the end utterly misleading accounts of what actually takes place. This, then, is the present net result of our discussion: We have the positive scientific clew to some and perhaps all the kinds of healing included under the terms mind cure, Christian Science, faith cure, etc.; and we find ourselves under peculiar obligations toward the evidence that is offered for such cures. What is now required is to define the known or probable limits of suggestive therapeutics, and then ask whether all that is verifiable in the practices just referred to can be included within those limits.

As to the visions that frequently accompany the healing work of faith, of shrines, etc., enough has been said to show how, under perfectly natural principles, they might occur to many a suppliant. All that is previously required is a considerable degree of suggestibility, a stock of active images of the saints, the Virgin, Christ, etc., emotional pressure, and intense concentration of attention for a considerable time upon divine things.

Limits of Mental Healing.

Medical men are pretty generally agreed that suggestion reaches directly none but functional disturbances; that is, disorders in which the organ remains intact but shows excessive, defective, or otherwise irregular activity. For example, ordinary constipation, biliousness, and indigestion are functional as contrasted with acute diseases like typhoid fever, and organic diseases, in which the organ is wholly or partly destroyed, as tuberculosis, cancer of the stomach, etc. Suggestion does not replace an arm shot off in battle; it does not set broken bones or reduce dislocations; it does not dislodge a cancerous growth and replace it with healthy tissue; it has no way of reaching a brain once in the grip of progressive senile dementia; it knows not how to kill or ex-

pel from the system the bacilli which cause so large
a proportion of diseases; nor can it claim to be an
antidote to any active poison. I am speaking here,
let it be noticed, of the prevailing medical view of
suggestion. Various systems opposed to medication deny that *their* methods are thus limited.
Whether this claim is just or no will be a question
for future inquiry.

But, while medical men assert that suggestion
reaches directly none but functional difficulties, they
do not fail to see that, even so, it may have an important indirect influence upon all classes of cases
whatever; for heightening or depressing the various
functions of nutrition, secretion, etc., determines for
good or ill the general basis upon which all medication and even surgery must rely. Or, to take the
very simplest case, if suggestion can assist a patient
to secure needed sleep, it thereby contributes a not
unimportant factor toward recovery. It is therefore not at all impossible that suggestion, through
its indirect connection with organic disease, should
now and then be the decisive therapeutic agent; that
is, that with which the patient recovers, without
which he does not. Suppose, for example, that a
tuberculous patient is led to have complete faith that
the Lord is going to heal him, or does now heal him.
One natural consequence would be a general toning
up of the system due to the new state of cheerfulness. This of itself would be something. But an-

other consequence would be that the patient would begin to act as though he were well; he would take exercise, thus bringing the uninjured parts of the lungs into action and improving the quality and the circulation of the blood. Now, it has happened again and again that a tuberculous lung has healed over through just such hygienic means as these. The destroyed part has not been restored, by any means, but absorbed and dried up. A determined will that sets one to mountain climbing or to sawing wood has done this, and there appears no reason why suggestion should not have the same effects. On the other hand, there is no reason to doubt that many a patient has died for the want of a proper mental attitude toward his disease.

Two facts, then, are established—that suggestion is a specific remedial agent in at least some functional disorders, and a general adjunct in all classes of medical and even surgical cases. When it should be exclusively employed; when it should be employed in connection with other treatment; how it should be employed in each case, whether through hypnosis or without hypnosis; what devices should be employed in each case to make the suggestion continuous and emphatic—these and all the other questions that concern the practical application of what has just been said must be left for answer to special medical literature and the personal skill of practitioners.

Two Misapprehensions.

From its very nature, of course, suggestion has its most pronounced effects upon disordered nervous functions. It is in constant employment in hospitals for diseased minds, and in the general duties of the skilled nurse everywhere. It is also recognized as one of the chief agencies at the disposal of the specialist in functional diseases of the nervous system. The large group of troubles allied to hysteria, the group of inebrieties (alcohol, opium, cocaine, tobacco, etc.), various difficulties of the sexual organism, and much more—these are a particularly favorable sphere for the employment of suggestion.

This recognized relation of suggestion to nervous disorders has produced a popular impression that the troubles reached by mental treatment are imaginary ones; that, for instance, if anyone seems to have been cured of rheumatism in this way, it was not real rheumatism that he had, and, indeed, that nothing was really the matter with him. But this is certainly an error. For, in the first place, pain hurts just the same whether its cause is a disturbed function of the mind and brain or the actual loss of some part of the bodily tissue. A headache brought on by grief or anxiety, or a diarrhœa caused by mental excitement, or indigestion resulting from nervous strain—all these are real enough; and even pain brought on simply by imagining pain is as genuine as any while it lasts. Again, it should be remembered that the nervous system participates in all the functions of all the organs. It is, as it were, the central telephone station, without which no subscriber can use even his own transmitter and receiver. Now, granting that suggestion has its direct effect upon the nervous system, we do not therefore shut up its efficacy to any one class of functions. Much less do we give it simply the task of removing diseases that are not there.

Another misapprehension is that suggestion is effective only with persons of weak or loosely organized mind. This prejudice totally misconceives the facts; for suggestibility is common in health as well as in disease in persons of both sexes, and in persons of all grades of mental power except the lowest. As before remarked, probably ninety per cent of the population, exclusive of infants, imbeciles, and the insane, can be hypnotized, under favorable conditions. Of course, some persons are far more susceptible than others, just as there are various degrees of response to all influences in nature. But that suggestibility does not connote mental weakness may be surmised from the fact that Sir Isaac Newton was highly suggestible.

The proof of this fact is contained in a letter of his written to John Locke, and dated June 30, 1691. In this letter Newton relates the following surprising experience that came to him in connection with some experiments on after-images of the sun: "At the third time, when the phantasm of light and colors about it were almost vanished [that is, when an after-image of the sun had almost vanished], intending my fancy upon them to see their last appearance, I found, to my amazement, that they began to return, and by little and little to become as lively and vivid as when I had newly looked upon the sun. But when I ceased to intend my fancy upon them, they vanished again. After this, I found that, as often as I went into the dark, and intended my mind upon them, as when a man looks earnestly to see anything which is difficult to be seen, I could make the phantasm return without looking any more upon the sun; and the oftener I made it return, the more easily I could make it return again. And at length, by repeating this without looking any more upon the sun, I made such an impression upon my eye [rather, on his mind] that, if I looked upon the clouds, or a book, or any bright object, I saw upon it a round bright spot of light like the sun, and, which is still stranger, though I looked upon the sun with my right eye only, and not with my left, yet my fancy began to make an impression upon my left eye, as well as upon my right. For if I shut my right eye, or looked upon a book or the clouds with my left eye, I could see the spectrum of the sun almost as plain as with my right eye, if I did but intend my fancy a little while upon it; for at first, if I

182

shut my right eye, and looked with my left, the spectrum of the sun did not appear till I intended my fancy upon it; but by repeating, this appeared every time more easily. And now, in a few hours' time, I had brought my eyes to such a pass, that I could look upon no bright object with either eye, but I saw the sun before me, so that I durst neither write nor read; but to recover the use of my eyes, shut myself up in my chamber made dark, for three days together, and used all means to divert my imagination from the sun. *For if I thought upon him, I presently saw his picture,* though I was in the dark. But by keeping in the dark, and employing my mind about other things, I began in three or four days to have some use of my eyes again, and, by forbearing to look upon bright objects, recovered them pretty well, though not so well but that, for some months after, the spectrum of the sun began to return as often as I began to meditate upon the phenomena, even though I lay in bed at midnight with my curtains drawn. But now I have been very well for many years, though I am apt to think, if I durst venture my eyes, I could still make the phantasm return by the power of my fancy." He closes the account by remarking that the power of the fancy is a knot too hard for him to untie.[1]

Now, that Sir Isaac Newton was able to give himself this hallucination of the sun by merely "intend-

<hr />

[1] Sir David Brewster, *Memoirs, etc., of Sir Isaac Newton*, i, 236ff.

ing" his mind upon the thought of the sun is not only not an evidence of intellectual weakness, but, on the contrary, it is a natural consequence of his marvelous power of analysis. It was his trained capacity for intense voluntary attention that gave his mere mental idea the character of a present sensation. It would therefore be a mistake to assume that only the weak-minded have anything to hope for in mental healing. It is true, of course, that the requisite concentration of attention may be secured through other than voluntary means; the mind of the simple may be overawed by a commanding personal presence and voice, or by fear of invisible influences near at hand, or through a properly arranged ensemble of exercises reaching their united climacteric in all-abounding faith. But a corresponding condition of susceptibility may be reached through rational conviction which justifies similar concentration of the mind—which is also the submission of the mind—upon the health-giving idea.

The Scientific Aspects of Faith Cure.

Under the term faith cure is here included not only what commonly goes under that name, but also the cures wrought at the shrines of saints, by relics, etc. In all these, it is clear, the subjective state of the patient, if a cure is to be wrought, must be one of intense faith. Now, such faith is already just the concentration of attention upon a health-giving idea wherein therapeutic suggestion consists; therefore, whether or no there is in faith cure anything more that the influence of suggestion, there is no denying that suggestion is actually operative therein. As a consequence, we are compelled to ascribe to suggestion all the cures of *functional* ailments wrought in the name of faith.

In general, there is a popular misapprehsion of the logic of the case. As a general rule, both believers and unbelievers in faith cure assume that the only alternatives are *all* and *nothing;* as though, if one case of faith cure fell outside the law of suggestion, all the other cases did also. This is certainly illogical. Principles must not be multiplied beyond necessity, and cases that can be explained by reference to an established natural law must be so explained. It follows that the question whether anything beyond suggestion is operative narrows itself down to the relatively few cases in which suggestion is not clearly seen to be adequate. There has been a great deal of hunting for cases of organic disease cured by faith, and what has seemed to be game has been started repeatedly, but the amount actually bagged is—one does not like to make a categorical denial of what depends upon the competence of others' observation, but it is safe to say at least this: that the defenders of faith cure have collected their test cases by methods that lack scientific precision, and that supposed proofs have been so uniformly exploded whenever trained physicians have examined them that the medical profession of to-day is entirely justified in ignoring the new announcements of miraculous cures made from time to time.

A favorite method of proving a miracle is to adduce evidence that competent physicians diagnosed a disease as organic, and then that it was removed by prayer. Obviously, the value of this reasoning depends on two assumptions: that the disease is really gone, and that the physicians who pronounced it organic were not mistaken. To make good the former assumption we ought to have competent diagnosis extending over a sufficient period to make assurance doubly sure; but to make good the latter we must give to physicians' opinions a degree of authority which they do not claim for themselves. The task of determining whether a given ailment is functional or organic is often extremely difficult, so difficult, in fact, that any candid physician admits his liability to error and is ready to correct and supplement his diagnosis by observing the course of the disease itself. Even if, in a given case, one or more physicians should be very positive, how should we determine in the end whether they were right or not? Suppose they themselves admitted that a miracle had been wrought; would even that sufficiently justify the assumption in question? A consideration of such points ought to bring us speedily back to the recognized criterion of scientific truth, namely, the general consensus of competent investigators in the given field. If, in addition to all this difficulty with the evidence, we take into consideration the fact, already admitted, that suggestion may be the decisive, though indirect, factor in curing even some organic diseases in some of their stages, we shall behold the already narrow margin of questionable cases shrinking away toward nothingness.

What keeps alive these beliefs, however, is the portion of truth that they contain, namely, the really marvelous extent and depth of the influence of suggestion. Without understanding the process, and therefore attributing it to occult powers, whether of mind, of spirits, of Satan, or of God, men have always employed suggestion for the causing, the prevention, and the curing of diseases. Bernheim says: "Therapeutic suggestion is not new; what is new is the methodical application of it, and its final adoption in general medicine."[1] Many apparently incredible tales are really worthy of acceptance to a certain degree. If a missing member is said to have been restored, or an emaciated person to have attained his normal weight in an instant, or a tuberculous lung to have been made whole, we may assume either that the facts have been exaggerated and distorted in the telling or

---

[1] *Suggestive Therapeutics*, 197.

else that the diagnosis was incorrect either before or after the cure; but it is scientifically credible that rheumatic cripples should go to a shrine on crutches and come away without them, and that bed-ridden women should arise and walk. On the same grounds, too, we are bound to accept the testimony to similar cures effected at the shrines of other religions than the Christian—before the feet of idols, by means of charms and amulets, and much more.

Professional faith healers, then, may work many genuine cures. All that is necessary is to work up confidence in one's gifts or abilities, and this can be done in various ways. Anything that will arouse the right state of mind in the patient will do. Paracelsus is said to have remarked that the statue of Peter will do as well as Peter himself provided only that the faith itself is as strong.[1] It is therefore possible for quacks, impostors, and men who do not understand their own powers to perform genuine cures. I once knew a pastor of a Protestant congregation who became a healer without intention on his part. The fact seems to be that he was so loved of his flock that his mere presence in the sick room or the mere touch of his hand came to have curative powers all unknown to him.

Understanding these things, the physicians of a certain hospital in Paris actually send scores of devout Catholics in the course of a year to the shrine

---

[1] Bernheim, 192.

of the Virgin at Lourdes. This leads to the remark
that Zola's novel *Lourdes* is, in general, a correct
description of the process of the mind in faith cure
and the like. The heroine of the tale injures her
back in girlhood and becomes a helpless woman, unable so much as to turn herself over in bed. All
ordinary medical treatment fails to restore her.
Only one possible help remains—she will make a
pilgrimage to the shrine at Lourdes. Possibly the
Virgin will have pity on her. Here follows an exceedingly skillful description of how hope is deep-
ened to faith, and how faith gradually intensifies
until it reaches a state of ecstasy and a self-induced
hypnotic trance in which the suggestion of walking
finally takes complete effect; but, from the inception
to the climax of the process, there is not one circumstance or force manifested which is not recognized
and made use of by the medical profession of to-day.

The Scientific Aspects of Christian Science.

Before proceeding to compare the medical work
of Christian Science with that of regular physicians
it is necessary, in the interest of clear thinking and
not less in the interest of fairness and neighborly
good will, to separate the various questions that
have been raised by this new system of religious
belief and practice. There are probably no religious movements that do not somewhere attach
themselves to the vital hunger of the soul for God

and bring to it some degree of satisfaction. The result is always a type of spiritual life and culture which, however incomplete it may be, nevertheless stands for some good. This is the reason why indiscriminate, wholesale denunciation of even fanatical sects rarely hinders their growth, much less extinguishes their influence. In the case of Christian Science, no one, it seems to me, who has candidly observed the type of spiritual life it tends to foster can fail to recognize in it some sure marks of the spirit of Christ. However erroneous its creed may be—and each Christian creed finds all the others more or less false—Christian Science may justly claim, by virtue of its ideal of life and by virtue of the type of life it actually tends to produce, that a place belongs to it among the denominations of Christians. Hence it is that tirades of general denunciation have thus far fallen so harmlessly upon it. Indeed, its head seems to have adopted the shrewd policy of assuming the attitude of those who are condemned without being understood. If, then, one were asked, What do you think of Christian Science? the wise answer would begin by distinguishing between the different aspects of the system.

In the first place, then, the system is both a theory and a practice. Its theory professes to be a system of purely rational metaphysics. On this side, therefore, the doctrine must be tested by the logical grounds adduced in its support. If this supposed metaphysics is truly rational, it must be able to win the assent, sooner or later, of persons trained in metaphysical thinking by a study of the history of philosophy. But, even if the theory is imperfect, this will not be the first time that good living has gone along with poor theology. On the side of practice, again, the system is twofold: it is a type of inner life, and it is a method of preventing and curing disease. It is with this last only that we are now concerned.

We might easily show defects in the metaphysical theory from which the mode of healing professes to be deduced, and thereupon be tempted to utter a generally adverse opinion. But is it not wiser to begin at the other end—first ask whether the method actually produces cures, and, if so, to what extent? As in the case of faith cure, the question will finally be, Is not suggestion probably an adequate explanation of the success actually attained by the method? We may grant without hesitation that Christian Science has taken hold upon some successful principle of healing. What is that principle, and what is the extent of its application?

It is surely significant that the rise of this system coincides in time with the last and greatest wave of scientific attention to hypnotism and mental therapeutics. Without questioning the sincerity of the account which Mrs. Eddy gives of the origin of her beliefs and practices, we can, nevertheless, be reasonably convinced of the real connection between them and the corresponding growth of scientific certainty concerning the facts and the law of suggestion. This will be plain to anyone who will compare the works of Mrs. Eddy with Tuke (1872) and Bernheim (1884). Indeed, it is doubtful whether she herself would claim anything more than that she has followed a given path *farther* than these authorities. Let us see whether, in fact, her methods—what is safe and successful in them—cannot be entirely accounted for as offshoots from regular medical science.

Tuke, when his tooth was being pulled, repeated to himself, "How delightful! how delightful!" The founder of Christian Science says: "We attack the belief of the sick in the reality of sickness, in order to heal them."[1] Again, she advises: "Mentally contradict every complaint from the body."[2] Medical science gives clear recognition to the fact that fear or expectation of disease tends to cause disease, and that the replacing of fear by cheerful states of mind is one means of restoration. Similarly, the founder of Christian Science says: "Always begin your treatment by allaying the fear of the patients. . . . If you succeed in wholly removing the fear, your patient is healed."[3] The last

[1] Mary Baker G. Eddy, *Retrospection and Introspection*, Boston, 1892, 76.
[2] *Science and Health*, Boston, 1896, 390.   [3] *Ibid.*, 43.

statement means no more than this: If you can get a patient to think that he is not in pain, he *is* not in pain; or, a pain of which we are not conscious is not a pain. This is equivalent to saying that where there is no painful consciousness there is no consciousness of pain—a proposition as useless as it is tautologous.

As far as can be ascertained from the evidence of publicly known fact, the limits of Christian Science healing are precisely the same as those recognized by the regular medical profession in the employment of suggestion. The founder of the system says: "Until the advancing age admits the efficacy and the supremacy of Mind, it is better to leave the adjustment of broken bones and dislocations to the fingers of the surgeon, while you confine yourself chiefly to mental reconstruction, and the prevention of inflammation and protracted confinement."[1] This is a most curious, not to say amusing, parallel. And the force of it is not broken by Mrs. Eddy's claim that she has cured "what is called organic disease as readily as she has cured purely functional disease;"[2] for the very same claim can be made for faith cure in all its forms and for the regular medical use of suggestion. The real question is not whether faith or Christian Science or plain suggestion has cured what are *called* organic diseases, but whether the diagnosis in these cases was correct both before and after the event. Until we are assured of such diag-

---

[1] *Science and Health*, 400.   [2] *Ibid.*, 43.

nosis, after as well as before the cure, we must assume that science—without a prefix—has probably defined the limits correctly. Furthermore, in the interest of human learning and human happiness, whoever knows of cases such as Mrs. Eddy claims to have cured should use every endeavor to bring them out of their obscurity into such light of publicity as will compel conviction.

It is to be hoped, in fact, that faith cure or Christian Science or something else will yet demonstrate all that is claimed as to the possibility of curing organic diseases so easily and quickly; yes, to set broken bones and reduce dislocations without recourse to physical manipulation! Who that loves his fellows would not hail with joy such a demonstration? Certainly science does not claim infallibility, nor does it pretend to say what is possible or impossible. It merely endeavors to give a correct analysis of observable facts. It is by analysis of such facts that the present view of the capacity of therapeutic suggestion has been reached, and nothing but further observation of the right kind of indubitable facts is necessary to bring about any degree of amendment.

Again, Christian Science treatment, in common with medical treatment, has various degrees of success and failure. Not infrequently it fails completely, even where the conditions seem to favor its success. This being so, the truly scientific attitude

of mind would require that the facts be more completely analyzed, so as to show what conditions were
present in the successful cases but absent in the
others. For faith curers to say that a patient failed
of a cure through lack of faith when the only evidence of such lack is that the cure did not occur, or
for Christian Scientists to claim a similar ground
for their own failures, is simply to beg the question.
Now, until such analysis of negative cases is forth-
coming from the believers in these systems we must
suppose that the real difficulty is in the practice
itself, and not in anything else whatever. Just
where the difficulty lies is plain enough to anyone
who understands the general facts of suggestion:
faith curers and Christian Scientists employ it upon
persons who are not readily suggestible, and in diseases in which it is inappropriate or inadequate.
That the adherents of these systems do not perceive
this to be the fact when they themselves fall victims
to their own imperfect practice would be astounding
if we did not take into account its entire consistency
with a method which proves the possibility of cure
by deduction instead of by induction. When you
deduce a consequence from a certainly known premise it is necessary to stand by it at all hazards. A
neighbor of mine was found by a caller hugging the
fire and nursing a cold. "O dear!" said she, "somehow I have let go!"

That such a system should find it impossible to

accept all the consequences of its own logic, however, is what might be expected. While the law of suggestion declares simply that physical functions tend to conform themselves to our ideas of them, Christian Science goes on to claim that we may so disbelieve in disease as not to suffer any pain due to any physical condition. It would logically follow that we could dispense with food, and this consequence Mrs. Eddy appears to have beheld; for she says: "It would be foolish to venture beyond our present understanding, foolish to stop eating until we gain more goodness and a clearer comprehension of the living God. In that perfect day of understanding we shall neither eat to live nor live to eat."[1] Yes, one may reply, it would be foolish to venture beyond our present understanding; but if the premises are so perfectly understood, how can the conclusion be obscure? How, unless our own inconsistency with facts is interpreted as inability to understand them? Not to press this point further, we may notice that here, again, as far as practice is concerned, medical science and Christian Science are in strange harmony. It is truly scientific to continue to eat until we know how to live without eating! And many who do not follow Mrs. Eddy believe with her that in the day of perfect understanding we shall neither eat to live nor live to eat!

All the probabilities are clearly in favor of the con-

---

[1] *Science and Health*, 387.

clusion that all the successes of Christian Science healing fall under the general law of suggestion. It differs from medical practice, however, in most important respects. First, being founded upon a process of deductive reasoning, or, rather, believing itself to be so founded, it is to that extent incapable of giving to observable facts their proper value. The theoretical basis, in other words, is sought by a mode of intellectual procedure outgrown and condemned since the age of Bacon. Second, as a consequence, it dispenses with diagnosis of a real sort; and, third, administers the same remedy to all persons and for all diseases! In thus employing a part for the whole it is not unlike the various quackeries that infest the land.

Of course, my neighbors point out the benefits that A, B, and C have experienced. But just the same kind of testimony can be had for almost any patent nostrum, not to mention the work of the regular physicians. Undoubtedly Christian Science is employing a curative agency that is of inestimable value in certain classes of cases, and of some value to everyone who wisely employs it in either health or disease. The crucial question is not whether this method succeeds, but rather whether it is being employed in a manner that secures the maximum of good results with the minimum of ill results. Here it would not be inappropriate to refer to the disastrous results that frequently attend Christian Science treatment, to say nothing of what would result if the general populace should once dare to intrust all ailments to it. But the distressing facts of failure, of needless death, even, have been too often spread before the public to need repetition here.

Meanwhile, it is worth noticing that the regular medical profession is to-day working wonders with suggestion no less astounding than those of Christian Science. If the growth of Christian Science has, as is claimed, stimulated physicians to the study of suggestion, let us be duly thankful. It is a principle with some of the great minds in medical science not to ignore irregular, homemade, and even quack remedies. But the more probable fact is that Christian Science has merely hastened a growth that was already started in the world of science and would of itself have sooner or later attained all that lay hidden in the principle. The facts that I am about to relate as illustrative of the wonders of suggestion were communicated to me directly by the physician concerned, and in the presence of the patient and her husband. The patient had submitted to an operation, but the wound had failed to heal. Suppuration set in, and continued until the patient despaired of life and was brought home to die. A new physician was now summoned, the one who tells me the tale. Suspecting that the difficulty had a nervous or mental root, he proceeded, little by little, without the use of medicines, to inspire hope in the patient's mind. He talked to her about the influence of the mind upon the body, even had her read passages on the subject from scientific books, taught her breathing, relaxation, and how to secure physical exercise though lying helpless in bed. In three weeks the wound was entirely dry, though medication other than ordinary bandaging had not been resorted to, and hypnosis had not been employed at all. Improvement was rapid from that point on, though one unfavorable circumstance occurred that seemed, nevertheless, to form the scientific climax of the case. Measles broke out in the family, the mother became anxious about the children, and the wound, already dry for some time, began once more to suppurate. Again it was closed by purely mental means together with the hygienic measures already mentioned, and no more setbacks occurred. In connection with this case, it is interesting to read another piece of advice given by Mrs. Eddy to her followers. She says: "To fix Truth steadfastly in your patients' thoughts explain Christian Science to them; but not too soon." Again: "Explain audibly to your patients (as soon as they can bear it) the utter control which Mind holds over body."[1]

If there were need of further illustrating what is common to medical practice on the one hand, and Christian Science and faith cure practice on the other, in so far, that is, as the latter succeed, it would

[1] *Science and Health*, 412, 415.

be possible to multiply many times instances scarcely less remarkable than the one just described. But enough has been said to show the common principle of all these different classes of healing without medication. The conclusion is that no one possesses a monopoly of this principle; that the effectiveness of the principle is utterly independent of the theological or metaphysical theories that sometimes accompany its use, and that, in the interest of the highest safety as well as effectiveness, its application requires scientific diagnosis, and, indeed, scientific observation and guidance from beginning to end.

Suggestion and Miracle.

Facts like those of suggestive healing have not failed to raise the question whether suggestion may not be the clew to the miraculous element in the lives of the saints, and even in the life of Christ, to say nothing of its bearing upon the wonder-working features of other religions. On the face of the stories of saintly visions, trances, and revelations, one can certainly read the imprint of auto-suggestion. Nor must we stop here. Let us consider two exclusive cases of the most strange physical manifestations that have been known to accompany spiritual exaltation. Seven hundred years ago St. Francis of Assisi, founder of the order of the Franciscans, after long meditation on the wounds of Christ, found upon his own person sores or "stigmata" corresponding to the five wounds of the Saviour. Similarly, in the third quarter of this century, Louise Lateau, a devout girl, repeatedly shed blood at the same points. A committee of competent investigators, after carefully examining into her case, became convinced that the phenomena were genuine, and free from intentional deception. But this very wonder has been duplicated in substance by one or more hypnotic subjects through whose skin blood has been caused to exude by suggestion. Lesser phenomena of the same class, such as the production of redness, inflammation, and swelling, have been repeatedly witnessed.

If all this should throw light upon some of the miracles of Christ, there would be no occasion for wonder. There appears no impropriety in his employing suggestion to the full extent of its therapeutic capacity. He made no claims not to do so. Furthermore, he did not in any way explain the *modus operandi* of his acts of compassionate healing. What is left to us, then, but to analyze these events as we would any others, and to accept the explanations of science as far as they go? This is not the place, even if the disposition were present, to give summary historical judgment upon the problems to which this mode of study would lead. Certainly much is recorded for which suggestion offers no explanation, but this should by no means deter us from applying this clew wherever it suffices, and trying it wherever there is the least prospect of success. Any fear that this would detract from his unique claims would simply misplace the accent of the whole Christian conception. It would turn attention from the Christ himself to physical phenomena. Against this very misplacement of accent Jesus himself explicitly protested. It would be in no degree derogatory to his character or to his claims of most intimate relations with the Father that he should employ the ordinary forces of nature and of mind. There is even collateral evidence in one case that this was the fact. The multitude of all sorts of sick folk who resorted to the pool of Bethesda—can there be any doubt that the kind of help they received was largely the same as that derived from the sacred pools one can see to-day in various parts of Europe? And if so, Jesus's word, taking the place of the pool, may justly be regarded as healing by the same means. We simply do not need to look any farther to find the explanation.

This leads to the remark that the very idea of the revelation of God in Christ is that of a divine possession and use of finite faculties. Neither in the life of Jesus nor in the prayers of any follower of his are we to assume a separation of natural from supernatural. To unfold all that this implies would carry us too far into philosophy and into the interpretation of the profoundest conceptions of Christianity. But this one word is offered in order to prevent the misassumption that the farthest possible application of scientific knowledge to any event, whether in our lives of trust and prayer or in the life of the Master, at all excludes, or puts away, or in any degree minimizes, those divine influences in which we live and move and have our being.

Hygienic and Therapeutic Value of the Christian Attitude toward Life.

If we may assume that the keynote of a normal Christian life is not the thought of sin, or of penitence, or of suffering, or of anxiety of any sort, but rather that of a joyous realization of the highest good, a realization begun now and growing ever toward greater fullness—if we may assume this, then it follows that the Christian mode of life tends directly toward physical health. Other things being equal, a religion that ruled by fear would have less robust votaries than one ruled by love. Faith, hope, and love are all full of constructive suggestion; for the first two take the attention away from present evil to present and future good; and love—the outgoing of self toward others for their own good—is the very antithesis of that brooding and self-contemplation whence grow the rankest weeds of unhealthful auto-suggestion. With persons of certain temperaments, if not of all, selfishness is distinctly unhealthful; and so it comes to pass that he who fails to use his health for the bettering of the world is in danger of losing even that which he hath.

It is remarkable how fully Jesus expressed the healthful state of mind in respect to God and his relation to our interests. "Be not anxious," "Let not your heart be troubled"—these are words of physical as well as spiritual healing. If we consider how, in spite of his own wondrous load of sorrow, he nevertheless with unremitting consistency painted life in colors the very opposite of all that is morbid, of all that is depressing; how, though he never blinded the eyes of his followers to the suffering they should endure for his sake, he taught them how to rejoice even in tribulation; and how perfectly all this fits one of the deepest physical as well as spiritual needs of the world—if we consider all this, we shall see new reason for calling him the Great Physician.

204

CHAPTER V

A Study of Spirituality

As long as men differ as profoundly as they do in temperament, education, occupation, and whatever else goes to shape a man's mode of reacting to the facts of life, there will be different types of religious experience. It becomes a matter of the greatest importance, therefore, to adjust religious training and religious exercises so as to appeal to the universally human in all these variations. What appeals to one man will not appeal to another. To adopt a homely old saw, "What's one man's food is another's poison." Emerson says:

> "I like a church; I like a cowl;
> I love a prophet of the soul;
> And on my heart monastic aisles
> Fall like sweet strains, or pensive smiles:
> Yet not for all his faith can see
> Would I that cowlèd churchman be.
>
> Why should the vest on him allure,
> Which I could not on me endure?"—*The Problem*.

There is, undoubtedly, something universal in religion, something adapted to all men, irrespective of temperamental and other peculiarities. When, however, one tries to say just what that something is, one's own temperament and environment are likely to tint one's statement. Nevertheless, the general religious consciousness of the world appears to be reaching the conclusion that Jesus grasped this universal principle and gave it a consummate expression in his statement of the law of love. Love to God and love to fellow-men—this is the universally attainable in religious experience. Yet even this law is liable to be misunderstood unless we go back to the Greek and observe that the verb translated "love" does not mean "be fond of," does not designate primarily a state of feeling, but a state of will, an attitude of mind that can be voluntarily assumed by all persons, irrespective of temperamental and other peculiarities.

In the course of ecclesiastical development, however, this universally human conception of the religion of Christ has been warped into special temperamental forms. What Jesus made so broad has been narrowed down to fit a particular kind of men, and temperamental differences have been mistaken for grades of spirituality. Following the fourfold division of temperaments, we may say that more than justice has been done to the melancholic and sanguine temperaments, and less than justice to the choleric. Or, pursuing the qualitative mode of classification, we may say that feeling has been unduly honored to the relative neglect of thought and, especially, of action.

It may conduce to clearness to give at this point a brief description of the four temperaments. The sanguine temperament, to begin with, is impulsive and impressionable. It responds promptly to the most heterogeneous influences and impulses; is full of feeling, ardent, hopeful, absorbed in the present; but its impressions and impulses are changeable and lacking in depth. The melancholic or, more properly, sentimental temperament is largely given to feeling and to feeling of a deeper and more lasting sort. It is introspective, tends somewhat strongly to unhappy moods, values the future above the present, and weighs everything by standards drawn from ideals that master the feelings. Next, the choleric temperament, in contrast with both these, is the temperament of action. Thought is not necessarily lacking in the melancholic temperament, but it does not tend so directly to practical issues as it does in the choleric. The choleric man is prompt, intense, perhaps impetuous. He looks without rather than within, and values the present above the future. He is likely to value consistency very highly, and his tendency is to be more intense than broad. The phlegmatic temperament, finally, is the slow one, the temperament of deliberation rather than of feeling or of impulse or of practical effectiveness. It must be understood, of course, that no one of these temperaments is often met with in its purity in any one person, although nearly everyone has a greater leaning in one direction than another. When our discussion speaks of persons of this or that temperament, therefore, the meaning is always persons whose mental organization is predominantly of the type named.

It has just been suggested that the development of ecclesiastical Christianity has tended to give more than their due to the sanguine and melancholic temperaments, and less than its due to the choleric. The evidence for this must now be offered. And first let us undertake a

Psychological Analysis of Sainthood.

If you will run over in your mind the qualities of mind and character which the Church, though hardly mankind in general, is most fond of contemplating, you will readily perceive that the specifically saintly qualities, in the traditional sense of sainthood, are almost exclusively states of feeling. A saint may have a strong intellect and vigorous will, but his claim to sainthood is not found in either of these. The saintly feeling may be either a quiet river, flowing through meadows of meditation toward the ocean of infinite love, or a mountain stream with many a thundering cataract; but feeling of one kind or another is the predominant quality.

Take St. Antony as an example. In Butler's *Lives of the Fathers, Martyrs, and Other Principal Saints,* we read that, at the age of twenty, Antony, listening to a sermon, heard the words, "Go, sell all that thou hast and give to the poor." He immediately applied these words literally to himself, and

with such impetuosity that the question is a legitimate one whether his act was not a product of suggestion pure and simple. He then became a recluse
and fled to the desert, where he gave himself up to
solitary contemplation and extreme austerities.
Here he passed through a remarkable inner drama.
Storm after storm of temptation swept over him.
At times the intensity of his feelings produced hallucinations: he heard the voice of Christ, was beat-
en by devils, was frightened by a specter of a black
boy, was enticed by a phantom woman.

The picture here is perfectly self-consistent, and
its explanation has been given in the last two chapters. Antony was a person of intense sensibility
united with a high tendency to mental automatisms.
He belongs to the same class as the persons in
Group I of Chapter III.

St. Francis of Assisi is perhaps the best example
of what the Roman Church means by a saint. The
instance of his extreme suggestibility given in the
last chapter has its setting in a highly emotional
temperament. We are told that he "communicated
[partook of the sacrament of the Lord's supper]
very often, and ordinarily with ecstasies in which
his soul was rapt and suspended in God." Often
while in prayer he fell into raptures. Contemplation of the sufferings of Christ brought on weeping so copious and prolonged as to ruin his eyes.
What it meant to him to have communion with God

is shown by a canticle which he composed on the love of Christ, a part of which is subjoined:

> "Into love's furnace I am cast;
> Into love's furnace I am cast;
> I burn, I languish, pine, and waste.
> O love divine, how sharp thy dart!
> How deep the wound that galls my heart!
> As wax in heat, so, from above
> My smitten soul dissolves in love.
> I live, yet languishing I die,
> While in thy furnace bound I lie.
>
> .   .   .   .   .   .
>
> In love's sweet swoon to thee I cleave,
> Bless'd source of love.
>
> .   .   .   .   .   .
>
> Love's slave, in chains of strong desire
> I'm bound.
>
> .   .   .   .   .
>
> Grant, O my God, who diedst for me,
> I, sinful wretch, may die for thee
> Of love's deep wounds; love to embrace,
> To swim in its sweet sea; thy face
> To see; then, joined with thee above,
> Shall I myself pass into love."

Protestants, of course, revert less to St. Francis than to an earlier man of God who, though he be the intellectual father of Western theology, is no less remarkable for the emotional side of his religious life. Augustine's *Confessions* clearly show that he was accustomed to indulge emotions for their own sake. Speaking of some of his youthful follies, he exclaims, "Who can unravel that twisted and tangled knottiness? It is foul. I hate to reflect on it. I hate to look on it."[1] But herein he probably misunderstands himself, for everything shows that he fairly revels in self-analysis. Hear how he dissects his feelings upon the death of a friend: "At this sorrow my heart was utterly darkened, and whatever I looked upon was death. My native country was a torture to me, and my father's house a wondrous unhappiness; and whatsoever I had participated in with him, wanting him, turned into a frightful torture. Mine eyes sought him everywhere, but he was not granted them; and I hated all places because he was not in them; nor could they now say to me, 'Behold, he is coming,' as they did when he was alive and absent. I became a great puzzle to myself, and asked my soul why she was so sad, and why she so exceedingly disquieted me. . . . Naught but tears were sweet to me, and they succeeded my friend in the dearest of my affections. And now, O Lord, these things are passed away, and time hath healed my wound. May I learn from thee . . . why weeping should be so sweet to the unhappy. . . . Whence, then, is it that such sweet fruit is plucked from the bitterness of life, from groans, tears, sighs, and lamentations?"[2] Again, describing the same experience, he says: "All things looked terrible, even the very light itself; and whatsoever was not what he was, was repulsive and hateful, except groans and tears, for in

---

[1] Book ii, chap. x.   [2] Book iv, chaps. iv and v.

those alone found I a little repose."[1] Here is a soul that not only feels profoundly, but also rolls his feelings under his tongue and secures satisfaction therefrom just because they are feelings. The connection between this trait and Augustine's besetting sin in his unregenerate days is plain enough.

There is, moreover, a direct connection between this temperamental quality and the characteristics of Augustine's religious experience. It is in exact keeping that an hallucination should accompany his conversion, and that, looking backward, we should find that his mother had repeatedly beheld visions.[2] After his conversion he still likes his food, but, looking upon all pleasures of sense as a temptation of the flesh, he examines himself with painful minuteness to see whether his only motive for eating is the preservation of health. The result is tribulation of soul, for he finds that he sometimes eats because he likes to, and so eats more than is absolutely necessary![3] Thus the passionate Augustine, always intemperate where feeling was concerned, was now intemperately temperate. The same thing happens with respect to the music of the Church. Of course such sensibilities as his could not help enjoying music, and so he must confess, "When it happens to me to be more moved by the singing than by what is sung I confess myself to have sinned criminally,

---

[1] Book iv, chap. vii   [2] Book iii, chap. xi; book v, chap. ix; book vi; chap. i.
[3] Book x, chap. xxxi.

and then I would rather not have heard the singing. See, now, the condition I am in! Weep with me, and weep for me, you who so control your inward feelings as that good results ensue."[1]

Citations like these do not, of course, discredit the piety of any saint. It is not at all for the purpose of detracting from anyone's reputation for holiness that the point has been raised, but rather for the sake of asking whether the saintly qualities that the Church has officially most delighted to honor do not presuppose temperamental traits possessed by only a part of humanity. Have not temperamental qualities been made a standard for measuring spirituality? The typical saint is the one who feels most—the one who feels the hollowness of the world or the awfulness of sin, who repents with strong groans and tears, who has great fervor in prayer, or a permanent mood of calm trustfulness, or ecstatic communion with the divine, or great billows of triumphant joy. Before such experiences can be common or characteristic there must be present, first of all, a mental organization of a particular kind. There are many, many persons who simply cannot feel the hollowness of the secular life that drove many saints to the desert. Only now and then do we find a person who can give himself up to meditation, prayer, self-examination, and the other spiritual exercises of the typical saint. I once

Typical Saint

---

[1] Book x, chap. xxxiii.

heard a theologian say that if he had an extremely important duty to perform in a very brief time he would spend the first quarter or half of the time in prayer. But, with the whole situation impelling one to be up and doing, persons of a more active nature simply could not spend so much time in real prayer. The very attempt to do so would seem to them to be a sacrilegious waste of time.

Spiritual Exercises.

It is only natural that this ideal of sainthood should color our spiritual exercises, or efforts after spiritual culture. This remark applies to the more mystical or, as it is sometimes called, devotional current in both Catholicism and Protestantism, and particularly, in our day, to Protestant Churches that put special stress upon what is called personal piety or personal religious experience. Here introspection and the cultivation of certain moods are held in especial esteem. When prayer is offered in a devotional meeting for a "personal blessing" what is really meant appears to be a comfortable religious emotion. As the term "blessing" is here commonly employed it would hardly include the perception of a new truth or a calm and deliberate decision to perform a duty. It may be asked, furthermore, whether the most common notion of Christian testimony is not that of witnessing to states of feeling.

Now, it is necessary to enter a loud *caveat* lest all this should be taken to be a denunciation of the cultivation of religious feeling. On the contrary, to seek to experience religious emotion, or, rather, to put one's self in the way of experiencing it, is as reasonable as any other part of religious aspiration. To take feeling out of religion would be as absurd as to take parental or conjugal fondness out of the family. Yet it is not possible to maintain the family solely, or even chiefly, by reliance upon feeling. What we protest against is one-sidedness; what we plead for is symmetry. Religion ought to rest upon and call into exercise all the faculties of the mind, and no superior sanctity should be ascribed to persons whose temperamental make-up is sentimental rather than choleric.

Professor James, remarking on the flabbiness of character that results from a disproportionate exercise of passive emotion, advises that we never so much as listen to a concert without compelling ourselves to perform also some voluntary act for the sake of preserving the equilibrium between sensibility and will.[1] When this equilibrium is lost in rushes a tide of religious vagaries. At a camp meeting in western New York a number of years ago a brother testified somewhat as follows: "Brethren, I feel—I feel—I feel—I feel that I feel—I can't tell you how I feel, but O, I feel! I feel!"

---

[1] *Principles of Psychology*, New York, 1890, i, 125f.

Not long since, the pastor of an important church made a remark to me substantially like this: "There are in my church two distinct classes of members. On the one hand, there is a group of substantial persons of high character and agreeable conduct who support the enterprises of the church with their money, but are rarely or never seen at prayer meeting. One never sees them prostrated before God in earnest prayer. If a sinner should come weeping to the altar they would not gather round to pray for him. If he should rise shouting they would shake hands with him and tell him they were glad he had started, but that is all. On the other hand, there is a class of members who can be relied upon to be present at the prayer meeting, who would rush to the altar to pray with a sinner, and who, if he should rise shouting, would scarcely know whether they were in the body or out of the body. Nevertheless, these persons are without influence in spite of their unction. They are flighty and changeable in their moods, lack organization, and their judgment is not to be trusted. If I were to go on a long journey I would not choose them for companions, but rather persons of the former description. And if I were to go sailing in a small boat I would not take one of these prayer-meeting members with me lest he should have a spell of some sort and capsize the boat." Without even guessing what he was doing, this pastor drew a firm line between two temperamental groups. On one side he ranged the members of his flock who manifest either the melancholic or the sanguine characteristics in excess, and confessed that the spiritual exercises of his church appealed almost exclusively to them. On the other side he ranged the more choleric and more balanced characters, against whom, it appears, there lies a suspicion of defective spirituality, and for no other reason than that they do not respond heartily to forms of church life and activity that are based upon a narrow and ill-balanced conception of the spiritual life.

Trace this temperamental line a step further and you will come upon the psychological root of what distinguishes holiness movements from the ordinary life of the churches. A holiness band or sect that separates itself from the general life of the church is organized and held together chiefly by temperamental affinities. This fact sets a rather strict limit to the possible growth of such movements, and goes far toward explaining their tendency to early dissolution. It is no more possible for the generality of Christians to attain the ecstasy or maintain the exalted serenity often proclaimed as their privilege than it is for them all to feel drawn toward the life of monks, nuns, and hermits. Anyone who doubts this statement would do well to observe how many seek for these experiences and how few attain them. Whether the honest seeker shall attain or not is simply a question of suggestibility and temperament.

The interest which many churches and pastors are now beginning to take in the social problems that agitate our times promises to do much toward removing the historical stigma upon the conception of spirituality. Men are beginning to perceive and to teach that merely filling one's station in life in the fear of God is a spiritual exercise. Doubtless one who is absorbed in the activities of what is called practical life has all the greater need for specific culture of the contemplative and emotional side of human nature; but it will be a great triumph for truth when the Church generally comes to believe and teach that the normal exercise of one faculty is neither more nor less a spiritual act than the normal exercise of any other faculty.

With the enfranchisement of the moral will we may expect also a recognition of the spiritual capacities of intellect. Perhaps the most typical illustration of the attitude of many religious minds toward the intellect is afforded by the distinction not seldom made between the devotional study of the Bible and the intellectual study of it. To say nothing of the confusion involved in the notion of a nonintellectual study of anything, we might ask whether truth has not a positive relation to religious devotion. We cannot admit the possibility that either untruth or the absence of truth concerning

the Bible can produce or promote any truly devotional state of mind. Surely, the followers of Him
who is the Truth, as well as the Way and the Life,
must see, upon reflection, that the impulse after
exact and complete knowledge of whatever may be
known is included in the most complete worship.
What a paradox it is that anyone who worships a
being of absolute wisdom, and looks for guidance
to the Spirit of Truth, should nevertheless exclude
intellectual exercises from the conception of the
spiritual life! Shall we not at last learn that we
may assume an attitude toward all truth that is itself essentially worship of the God of Truth? A
prominent philosopher of our day has put one aspect
of the matter in these profoundly true words: "All
of us, I presume, more or less are led beyond the
region of ordinary facts. Some in one way and
some in others, we seem to touch and have communion with what is beyond the visible world. In
various manners we find something higher which
both supports and humbles, both chastens and trans-
ports us. And, with certain persons, the intellectual
effort to understand the universe is a principal way
of thus experiencing the Deity."[1]

Some Psychological Aspects of Hymnology.

Song proceeds from emotion as one of its most
natural and adequate expressions. It returns to

---

[1] F. H. Bradley, *Appearance and Reality*, 5f.

emotion, also, as its quickener and inspirer. We should expect sacred music, then, to be full of religious feeling; and the test of its quality will be just its capacity to communicate in fitting literary and musical form the various chords, major and minor, that resound throughout normal religious experience. Should it omit to echo some of these chords, or vary too little from some one or a few favorite chords, in either case it would be defective itself or significant of defect in ecclesiastical life. It is reasonable to look to the hymns sung by any Church for an index, true though partial, of the emotional aspect of its life. If we find certain types of sentiment unrepresented in the hymns, we infer that the corresponding type of religious experience has not been sufficiently cultivated to secure proportional musical expression.

It must be remembered, too, that emotion has a scale as large and as varied as human life itself. When we speak of emotional temperament, emotional novels, emotional religious meetings, and the like, what we really have in mind is not merely the abundance of emotion, but also the quality. A tale of heroic action, for example, may stir the reader fully as much as a tale of suffering, but only the latter would ordinarily be called emotional. Just so, every normal religious activity has its own appropriate emotional coloring, but not every form of religious life would be popularly called emotional.

In any attempt at a psychological analysis of hymnology, therefore, it is necessary to note what emotion, rather than what degree of emotion, comes to expression. In particular, in the present instance we need to know whether, as in the most approved spiritual exercises, the point of view tends to be that of feeling for its own sake or that of feeling as the atmospheric coloring of a many-sided consciousness. More specifically, is the point of view that of introspection, subjectivity, self-consciousness, or that of practical activities and interests and facts?

Bearing this distinction in mind, let us examine the first Hymnal that comes to hand, that of the Methodist Episcopal Church. Possibly the scope of its contents will scarcely correspond with the scope of the hymns most frequently in actual use; and yet any such depository of the ages will surely reveal something as to the question before us.

The Methodist Hymnal contains, to begin with, 81 hymns on the subject of Christ. Of these 15 have to do with his incarnation and birth, 21 with his sufferings and death, 37 with his resurrection, priesthood, and reign, and only 8 with his life and character; that is, only one in ten of the hymns about Christ have to do with his life and character. Moreover, of these eight, three deal with the transfiguration, one deals with his patience, one with his meekness, one with his tears, one speaks of him as a present help, one treats a miracle of healing as a spiritual type. Not one has for its topic Jesus's life activities objectively considered. His life was certainly not devoid of stirring action, or of deeds fit to inspire poetic eulogy. Why, then, are his passive virtues almost the only ones to be noticed? Doubtless because the mind of the Church, through historical causes yet to be named, has never fully awaked to see the breadth of that which constitutes the divine-human life.

Again, this Hymnal contains 345 hymns on the general topic of the Christian, but only 47, or less than one in seven, treats of Christian activity. This is surely significant, but it is far from being the end of the matter. For Christian activity can be considered in either one of two ways: we may fix our thought upon the thing to be done, or upon the feelings that accompany the doing of it. We may assume the standpoint of the Epistle of James, or that of the First Epistle of John. Take, for example, this stanza of Henry Alford's hymn, "Forward! be our watchword," and notice how the attention is directed to the contemplated act:

> " Forward ! flock of Jesus,
>   Salt of all the earth,
> Till each yearning purpose
>   Spring to glorious birth :
> Sick, they ask for healing ;
>   Blind, they grope for day;
> Pour upon the nations
>   Wisdom's loving ray.

Forward, out of error,
  Leave behind the night;
Forward through the darkness,
  Forward into light!"

This stanza does not lack feeling, but never once does the feeling become the object thought about or aimed at.

Compare with this Watts's hymn, "Am I a soldier of the cross?" This also is a hymn of Christian activity, but the attention is turned in just the opposite direction—to the fears, the blushes, the courage that is needed; to bearing the toil, enduring the pain; to the foretaste of victory even in the midst of the fight. The battle of faith is looked at solely from the standpoint of the fighter's feelings, and not a word is breathed about the aims which Christian warfare seeks to accomplish. The subjective, introspective mood is all-controlling.

The same attitude is, if possible, even more vividly revealed in several of Charles Wesley's hymns of Christian activity, as, for instance, "A charge to keep I have." Another excellent example may be found in his hymn, "Lo! I come with joy:"

"Lo! I come with joy to do
  The Master's blessed will;
Him in outward works pursue,
  And serve his pleasure still.
Faithful to my Lord's commands,
  I still would choose the better part,
Serve with careful Martha's hands,
  And loving Mary's heart.

.   .   .   .   .

> Careful, without care I am,
>   Nor feel my happy toil,
>   Kept in peace by Jesus' name,
>   Supported by his smile."

Perhaps the best example of all is the fourth stanza of his hymn, "Son of the carpenter, receive:"

> "Careless through outward cares I go,
>   From all distraction free :
>   My hands are but engaged below,
>   My heart is still with thee."

In this entire group of hymns the attention is directed, you perceive, not at all to the specific end in view, nor to the specific means of attaining it, but to the feelings that one may experience in connection with unspecified activities and difficulties.

Once more permit the remark that the antithesis here pointed out is not to the discredit of these introspective, subjective expressions of religious activity. Many of them are beautiful, inspiring, and fit to be sung forever. This is one perfectly legitimate side of religious sentiment. But it is only one side, and that is the whole point—unless one should find also that thinking of one's feelings is an easy road to a selfish, unsocial, and hence unchristian view of life. One thing, at least, ought to be clear, and that is that the sentiments natural to the more objective, self-forgetting attitude demand utterance fully as much as those just described.

It is therefore somewhat remarkable to find that of the entire 47 hymns on Christian activity, 32 treat their theme in a purely subjective way, only 9 in a purely objective way, while 6 are mixed or indeterminate.

Again, this Hymnal contains 182 hymns on the Church, of which only 89, or a trifle less than one half, have to do with any species of Church work. These 89 are divided about equally among the following subjects: Erection of Churches, Children and Youth, Charities and Reforms, and Missions. It is, naturally, less easy to follow the cleavage plane between the subjective and the objective mood through these topics than through that of Christian activity. Erection of Churches, and Missions, moreover, present clear objective images for contemplation. The objective attitude could scarcely be escaped. The test comes when the topic concerns our own present life in the world; hence particularly with the hymns on Charities and Reforms. Of the 18 hymns in this group only 8 are clearly of the objective variety.

Putting together the results of examining these various sets of hymns, we have a striking exhibit:

Number of hymns in the entire collection.... 1,117
Number of hymns on Christ, the Christian, and the Church........................ 608
On Life and Character of Christ, Christian Activity, and Church Work............ 144
On the Life Activities of Christ, Christian Activity, and Charities and Reforms, all objectively viewed.................... 17

In other words, less than twenty-four per cent of the hymns on Christ, the Christian, and the Church have to do with the life and character of Christ, Christian activity, and Church work. Again, less than three per cent of the said hymns on Christ, Christian, and Church treat of the life activities of Christ, Christian activity, and charities and reforms in an objective spirit. Finally, it follows that, of the entire collection, only about one and a half per cent take up the practical problems of the everyday activities of the adult Christian in this spirit.

It is not necessary to suspect that falsehood has crept into the ideals of life here presented except as one-sidedness implies partial truth. Far be it from me to discourage the singing of the tender and noble sentiments that assuage the griefs of life and lighten its burdens. Yet it would be folly to ignore the existence of many Christians whose deepest soul remains unuttered even through these beautiful products of the subjective mood. Without doubt many persons can actually feel with Charles Wesley that only the hands are engaged below, while the heart is elsewhere; but, on the other hand, there are men, and not a few of them, whose hearts go into their earthly work with their hands. These are particularly the persons whose temperament we describe as choleric. They are less interested in how their surroundings impress them than in controlling those surroundings; they are not without feeling, but their primary need is for action, and their characteristic feelings are the desires and enthusiasms, disappointments and joys of intense purpose; they are eager, earnest, persistent; they think of the present rather than of the future, of the near rather than of the remote; and their glance is outward rather than inward. The mind of such a person is taken up with the thought of ends and of means; upon these his feelings as well as his tongue and his hands fix themselves. His happiness lies not in tranquillity, not in contemplation of heaven or of the privileges of the Gospel, but rather in seeing things move. Now, while this type of mind needs, perhaps, to be turned in upon itself now and then, it also needs self-expression which the vast majority of the hymns referred to cannot provide. These hymns appeal rather to the melancholic temperament, which is given to feeling rather than to action, to contemplation of ideals rather than of means and ends, to future rather than present good, and to subjective rather than to objective standards for the measurement of values.

Without undertaking the ungracious as well as ungrateful task of dictating inspirations to poets, we may, nevertheless, venture to describe a need in hymnology. For, assuredly, poetry does enter into the dynamics of our life, and why should it not add its power to whatever in life is worth striving for? Truth and goodness and beauty can never be so separated in reality as to make art entirely superfluous at any point. Our greatest present unfulfilled need seems to be poems of social goodness. Understanding religion to be essentially love to God and love to man, and understanding love to be a matter of the will as well as of sentiment—the basis of the family and of society—we may say that we need the dynamics of a poetry of active love. And this in no narrow sense, such, for instance, as is connoted by the traditional use of the term "charity." For the immanence of God in the whole of nature and of human life, together with the supremacy—nay, adequacy—of love as a motive for life in all its ramifications, lifts the whole of life out of the dust and into the clear air and sunlight of beauty. One can even find it in one's heart to sympathize with eccentric Professor Blackie, who sings to God as the God of glee.[1] Much more, then, is it true

> "That, in a world, made for whatever else,
> Not made for mere enjoyment—in a world
> Of toil but half-requited, or, at best,
> Paid in some futile currency of breath,"[2]

we need the voice of song to transfigure all into that beauty which is the truth of things. We need songs *ad rem,* infusing love—the interpreter, the fulfiller of the law—into the occupations of hand and of brain. Indeed, when we learn what it means to do all to the glory of God will not the consciousness

---

[1] *Songs of Religion and Life,* New York, 1876, 60.
[2] Lowell, " The Cathedral "

of the divine presence inevitably break forth into song?

The Spirituality of Prayer-Meeting Songs.

If we turn, now, from the recognized hymns to the popular revival, prayer-meeting, and Sunday-school songs, we shall find a slightly different species of one-sidedness. Feeling is still in the ascendency, but it is of a mobile and superficial kind. There is nothing of the profound emotion and stately movement of the standard hymns. The water is shallow, and light and shifty winds raise ripples everywhere upon its surface. I speak now particularly of the psychological effect of the musical compositions. Instead of the solemn procession of those who ascend into the hill of the Lord, to stand in his holy place, we have a mere hop, skip, and jump, or a game of tag. The thought is equally weak and disconnected. There is no foresight, hindsight, or proportion, and no sense of consistency. What is intended for thought is a mere jumble of pious ideas. The composition of the verse corresponds. It is purely mechanical. Meter is held in light esteem, and any crime against sense or syntax is committed for the sake of making rhymes.

Here and there in these popular collections are songs worthy of better company, but the class as a whole tends to the type just described. As an example, I will take, not the worst, but the best, of the recent revival songs that have come to my attention—"Let Him In:"

> "There's a stranger at the door,
> He has been there oft before;
> Let him in ere he is gone,
> Let him in, the Holy One,
> Jesus Christ, the Father's Son.

> "Open now to him your heart;
> If you wait he will depart.
> Let him in, he is your friend,
> He your soul will sure defend,
> He will keep you to the end.

> "Hear you now his loving voice,
> Now, O, now make him your choice;
> He is standing at the door,
> Joy to you he will restore,
> And his name you will adore.

> "Now admit the heavenly Guest,
> He will make for you a feast.
> He will speak your sins forgiven,
> And when earth ties all are riven,
> He will take you home to heaven."

You perceive that the thought and composition, especially after the first stanza, are decidedly patchy. With the omission of two "ands," the second, third, and fourth stanzas could be read in the inverse order of the lines as well as in the order given. More than that, leaving out the last two lines—the only ones having any obvious rhetorical connection—we could take the remainder, write one line on each of thirteen slips of paper, shake the slips in a hat, draw them out indiscriminately, and, taking them in the new order, have nearly, if not quite, as good a poem as the one before us. And yet this composition is probably less open to serious objection than the majority of the songs of its class.

This analysis has been made, not in the interest of art, whether musical or rhetorical, nor even in the interest of logic, but solely to raise the question whether these popular sacred songs do not express and appeal to a particular temperament rather than to the heart of humanity as a whole. Surely only a fraction of those who need comfort, inspiration, or conversion can respond to such invitations as that just analyzed, and yet this is the kind with which we are trying to draw the whole world to Christ.

Lotze has called attention to a parallel between the four temperaments and four ages of man's life. The sanguine temperament, he says, corresponds to childhood, the melancholic (which he calls the sentimental) to youth, the choleric to maturity, and the phlegmatic to old age. We have just seen that the tendency of too many of the standard hymns of the Church is to express the sentimental temperament. It is now even more obvious that our popular revival songs correspond to the sanguine temperament. The sanguine personality is characterized less by depth of feeling than by ready response to every kind of impression. Rapid changes from one mood or activity to another are common. Impressions predominate over action. The sanguine person lives in the present rather than the future, and tends to cheerful rather than to serious moods. Now, do you not see that these traits exactly describe the songs in question? They are mere fleeting impressions, and lack continuity and consistency. In other words, they tend toward childishness.

Popular Notions of Spirituality.

In order to pursue still further the hypothesis that a certain psychological one-sidedness pervades much of what is called spiritual life, I have undertaken to make a direct analysis of the notions of spirituality entertained by a considerable group of persons. To a large class of college students, chiefly seniors, I made the following oral requests: "First, think of some one whom you would call spiritual in the religious sense. Let it not be Christ or one of the apostles. Then [after a pause], write down, without revision or criticism, what it was in that person that seemed to show his spirituality."

The exercise was entirely impromptu, and the whole process consumed only a few minutes. The purpose of the exercise was to get at the actual working notions of spirituality rather than at theories of what ought to be called by that name. Hence a concrete object was brought before the mind, and the first impression was recorded. Seventy papers were received, but enough of them named more than one quality to raise the number of specifications to 109. We have, then, 109 specifications of what is spontaneously looked upon as constituting spirituality by 70 college students. The qualities specified and the number of times each was named may be exhibited as follows:

1. The physical man, such as Christlike face, shining face, eyes that seem to see things not of this world, etc................ 9
2. Otherworldliness, such as not of this world, given up the world, absorbed in God, thinking of life to come, etc........... 7
3. Passive virtues, such as gentleness, peace, even temper, meekness, humility, patience, trust, cheerfulness............. 11
4. Communion with the divine, living near God, thinking about God, reverence.... 6
5. Religious exercises, such as faith in prayer, delight in prayer, interest in spiritual things or in religious exercises........ 9
6. Beautiful personality, beautiful character, Christlike spirit 3
7. Scattering: love of nature, love of Bible, fervor of religious feeling, excessively conscientious 4
8. Social feeling and activity, such as unselfishness, living for others, sympathy, charitable, kind, influence for good........ 24
9. Daily life, consistent Christian living..... 7
10. Truthfulness, sincerity, hatred for wrong, ideal conception of character, high character, something that attracted one.... 6
11. Fidelity to duty, loyalty to God, sense of duty, earnestness in religious work or in everything 9

The largest single group in this list is that of social feelings and activities. This is, doubtless, a sign of a healthful trend of thought in our colleges. Yet, on the other hand, the proportion in which social virtues here come to recognition is not what we should expect from persons who have learned from Him who revealed to us the meaning of life as summed up in love. It will be noticed that the first seven groups in the table form one consistent set, while the remaining groups form another and contrasting set. In the former we have otherworldliness, passive virtues, the contemplative life, and spiritual exercises. In the latter the altruistic feelings, the active virtues, and intellectual qualities are gathered together. The former set contains 49 specifications, the latter 60. In all probability the proportions would be changed if we could only know what was in the minds of writers who mentioned religious work, enthusiasm in religious work, speaking of religious things, exhorting, etc. These expressions may represent the active life less than they do emotion and contemplation. Yet even as the two sets of groups stand they reveal an interesting state of the popular mind. Here are seventy young persons who have drunk not merely of the average religious teaching, but also of the newer spirit which puts emphasis upon the social virtues; yet it appears probable that, for every six times that these persons think of either the altruistic feelings, the active virtues, or intellectual qualities as constitutive of spirituality, they think of something negative, passive, introspective, or private five times.

Furthermore, of the 70 papers, 24 mentioned not one of the altruistic, active, or intellectual qualities. When we realize that under these three terms are included not only what is sometimes called mere morality, etc., but also religious work, kindness, sincerity, consistency, sense of duty, and even influence for good, the result becomes little less than astounding.

It will be recalled that the directions to the writers of these papers were to think of some spiritual person and then name the quality in which the spirituality manifested itself. A third request was to say whether the spiritual person thought about was a man or a woman. Of the 70 writers, 36 were men and 34 women. But 40 of the writers thought of a woman, and only 30 of a man, as a type of spirituality. The distribution of the answers is as follows: Of the 36 men returning answers, 21 thought of a

man, and 15 of a woman. Of the 34 women returning answers, 9 thought of a man, and 25 of a
woman. Thus there appears to be a clear tendency
for the men to think of a man as representing spirituality, but a much more pronounced tendency for
women to think of a woman. This may or may not
be very significant, for the number examined is too
small to base a generalization upon. But it at least
suggests a most significant question, that of the relation of masculine to feminine qualities in Church
life and Church ideals.

The "Eternally Feminine" in the Church.

It has not escaped popular observation that there
is some sort of difference between the religious life
characteristic of women and that characteristic of
men. Women are commonly said to be more religious than men, but I think it can be shown that
the real difference is less in the degree of religiousness than in the general make-up of the mind. Sex
is certainly a fact of mental as well as of physical
constitution, and the mental peculiarities of each
sex naturally and necessarily appear in religion as
well as elsewhere. Two of the best established
general differences between the male and the female
mind are these: first, the female mind tends more
than the male to feeling; and, second, it is more
suggestible.[1]

---

[1] Havelock Ellis, *Man and Woman*, London, 1898, chaps. xii, xiii.

Granted that this generalization is correct, what religious differences should we expect to find between the sexes? We should expect that women brought up under continuous religious incitement and suggestion would exhibit greater continuity in religious feeling and less tendency to pass through religious crises. And this is, in fact, what we appear to discover. With men religion tends more to focus itself into intense crises. Women yield sooner and show more placid progress, while men pass through more definite periods of awakening.

One of the very striking things about the religious autobiographies presented to me is that, while religion seems to be a sort of atmosphere in the life of women—something all-pervasive and easily taken for granted—with the men it is more sharply defined, brings greater struggles, and tends more to climacteric periods. Men are more likely than women, it appears, to resist certain religious tendencies up to the point of explosion.

The following facts gathered by Starbuck illustrate this general view: The storm and stress period, the period of doubt, struggle, etc., is of shorter duration with women than with men.[1] Again, men display more friction against surroundings, more difficulty with points of belief,[2] more doubt arising from educational influences,[3] more

---

[1] Growth, *American Journal of Psychology*, ix, 84.
[2] *Ibid.*, Table V.   [3] *Ibid.*, Table VI.

readiness to question traditional beliefs and customs,[1] more pronounced tendency to resist conviction, to pray, to call on God, to lose sleep and appetite—in a word, to experience the more turbulent manifestations. Women, on the other hand, show greater tendency to the less intense emotions, such as depression, sadness, meditativeness, humility, sense of helplessness.[2] Again, among Starbuck's cases, twice as large a proportion of men as of women were converted at home, and generally alone, while six times as many women as men were converted at the regular church services. This shows the greater dependence of women upon external suggestion.[3] Furthermore, the disturbances are greater for the women in the nonrevival cases, in which external suggestion is relatively lacking, but for the men in the revival cases, in which it is most abundant.[4] Thus women go more easily with the tide, while with men questions of religion go deeper—more deeply, that is, into the region of clear self-consciousness, decision, initiative.[5] Finally, men tend more than women to regard forgiveness and divine aid as central in their conversion.[6]

From the cases I have myself examined I am able to add some further facts. Thus, while the two

---

[1] Growth, Table VII, *American Journal of Psychology*, ix.
[2] Conversion, Table V, *American Journal of Psychology*, viii.
[3] *Ibid.*, Table I. [4] *Ibid.*, Table V. Comp. Growth, Table V.
[5] *Ibid.*, Table VII. [6] *Ibid.*, Table VI.

sexes report practical doubts—that is, doubts of their personal religious status—in about the same proportions, more than twice as many men as women report theoretical doubts—that is, doubts concerning doctrines. Again, among those who definitely sought for a striking transformation, the proportion of those whose expectation was completely satisfied is decidedly greater among the women than among the men. Once more, in response to a question as to what was found permanent in their religious experience, nearly every woman who gave an answer mentioned some kind of satisfactory feeling, while less than half of the men did so. Moreover, men were alone in mentioning forgiveness or anything connected with it, and almost alone in mentioning anything connected with right or wrong.[1]

All this goes to show that women respond to religion more feelingly, and in some respects more continuously, but men more energetically and with a higher potential of self-conscious reflection and choice. With women religion is more like the intuitive tact that helps them so much in all the relations of life; with men it requires the clumsier instruments of deliberation. Any attempt, therefore, to determine which sex is the more religious would simply end in a dispute as to the relative rank of different sets of faculties.

---

[1] See pp. 252f.

Our results may be summarized and exhibited as follows:

RELIGIOUS TRAITS OF MEN AND OF WOMEN COMPARED.

Men.	Women.
Intellect more prominent; hence, more theoretical doubts.	Sensibility more prominent; hence, doubts of personal status, but relatively few theoretical doubts.
Emotion focuses on definite objects and at definite periods; hence, more turbulent.	Emotion more constant, more diffused, more gentle.
Less suggestible, resist more, have more intense struggle, and less fulfillment of expectation. Attain more in solitude.	More suggestible; yield more readily to ordinary influences; attain less in solitude; have less intense struggle, and more fulfillment of expectation.
Active virtues more prominent.	Passive virtues more prominent.

It should be said that the evidence for this conclusion rests not merely upon the relatively few cases that I have examined, but upon all the results thus far gathered in this particular field. The strength of the conclusion lies in the fact that all lines of investigation converge upon the same point.

It would be interesting to know, if possible, just what psychical forces, as distinguished from doctrinal reasonings, have given the Virgin Mary the place she holds in the worship of Christendom. In any case, we shall not go far astray by assuming that Mariolatry is, among other things, an effort to provide in the object worshiped certain gentler qualities that are more characteristic of the female sex than of the male. The same impulse has led religious persons here and there, and occasionally a

whole sect, to teach the doctrine of the motherhood
as well as fatherhood of God. These gentler qualities we may, for convenience' sake, designate under
the single term "compassion."

There is no reason to doubt that the act of worship, on the part of imperfect creatures like ourselves, requires for its highest perfection some conception or sense of compassion felt by God toward
his worshiper. When Spinoza proposed a kind of
love for God that made no demands upon God for a
sympathetic response he proposed something that
has never met the needs of man and never can meet
them. We may, indeed, assert, and glory in the
assertion, that Christianity has brought into worship and religious life generally a feminine element.

But when this instinctive demand of human nature, instead of expressing itself as Jesus expressed
it, sought satisfaction in the worship of Mary
normal proportions were destroyed. Feminine
qualities came to outweigh the masculine in the prevailing conception of divinity, and, of course, feminine virtues came to outweigh masculine in the
Church's ideal of the good life.

Nor has Protestantism wholly cleared itself from
this moral obscuration. In theory we reject the
worship of Mary; but in practice do we not still hold
the passive virtues in disproportionate esteem? I
am inclined to think that Romanes did not belie the
common thought when he wrote these words: "But

when the ideal was changed by Christ—when the highest place in the hierarchy of the virtues was assigned to faith, hope, and charity, to piety, patience, and long-suffering, to forgiveness, self-denial, and even self-abasement—we cannot wonder that, in so extraordinary a collision between the ideals of virtue, it should have been the women who first flocked in numbers around the standard of the cross." "The whole organization of woman is formed on a plan of greater delicacy, and her mental structure is correspondingly more refined; it is further removed from the struggling instincts of the lower animals, and thus more nearly approaches our conception of the spiritual."[1] It is the same understanding, or rather misunderstanding, of the round sphere of Christian principle that induces Brinton to define the cardinal principle of the Christian faith as "the holiness of suffering and self-abnegation."[2]

That this feminine element has an essential part in the Christian ideal of life is one of the glories of Christianity. A feminine element is as necessary to religion as woman is to the life of the species. *But,* in the spiritual as in the natural realm, whatever tends to isolate this element tends also to make it barren and unfruitful. Neither the man alone nor the woman alone is a perfect type, but rather the family, in which the two complementary qualities

[1] " Mental Differences between Men and Women," in *Essays*, London and New York, 1897, 123, 125 ; also in *Nineteenth Century* for May, 1887.

[2] *Religions of Primitive Peoples*, New York, 1898, 181.

are balanced the one over against the other. The practical question that results from this view is whether the Church is to be simply a Sister of Mercy or preferably a family. Is its mission any more that of sympathy, or even of salvation in the narrower sense of this term, than it is such active participation in the world's work as shall constitute the whole of human life an incarnation of the divine? And our saints—are they to be distinguished from other human beings by sex and temperament, or by something more divine?

Some Results of a Temperamental Interpretation of Christianity.

Including under the one convenient term "temperament" all the differences of sex and individuality discussed in this chapter, we may now ask whether the proposition with which we started has not been abundantly made out—the proposition, namely, that Jesus' simple and universally human conception of spiritual life has been warped into particular temperamental forms in organized Christianity. This has been shown by an analysis of sainthood as traditionally understood; of prevalent spiritual exercises; of our hymns and songs; of popular conceptions of spirituality, and, finally, of the historical influence of Mariolatry. The conclusion upon which all these diverse lines of investigation converge is that organized Christianity in general, Protestant as well as Catholic, places insufficient value upon the more masculine, active, or practical qualities of goodness; or, to speak in directly psychological terms, that the forms of religious life natural to the choleric temperament are habitually discounted in favor of those natural to the sanguine and melancholic temperaments, particularly the latter.

The results, which are at the same time a part of the evidence that the diagnosis is accurate, are comprised in the group of facts presented again and again as churchmen have asked whether the Church of to-day can yet adjust itself to modern life. There is, in the first place, the much-deplored disproportion of the sexes in our Church life. It is due, very likely, to several causes. It may be said, for instance, that men, since they are under greater industrial and economic pressure than women, have less time for worship and other religious exercises. But, even if this is so, we may yet be confident that a demand of our nature as profound as the religious instinct is never balked merely by lack of time for indulging it. Hungry men will take time or make time to eat. These very men who feel the pressure of life's conflict find time for many things outside of business. Witness, for example, the luxuriant growth of clubs, mutual benefit insurance societies, secret orders, and other social agencies, at the very time when it is so hard to get men to go to church.

At the very period, too, when the workingman's day has been generally lowered from ten to nine or eight hours the Church finds herself increasingly incapable of commanding any part of the workingman's time. Moreover, even if it be true that the heavy hand of worldly responsibility keeps men back from the Church, what is this but a confession that the Church is unable to compete with the world? Or, if this be too narrow a view to take of social forces—and religious forces, too—let us ask whether the glory of religion should not shine as much in days of adversity and struggle and work as in days of placid contentment. Are religion and the Church, after all, something for men's leisure hours?

Another possible explanation of the indifference of men toward the Church is that there is a greater tendency for men than for women to be dissatisfied with the attitude of the Church toward industrial problems and movements. Here again, even if we grant the premises, the explanation is seriously lame and incomplete. For why have not these dissatisfied men asserted themselves in the life of the Church by preventing or reversing the condition complained of? They are in the majority; why have they not outvoted those with whom they disagree? It is a matter of the deepest regret that the masses should be alienated, but it is cause for profound alarm that they do not seem to feel their loss. There's the rub.

Unless we adopt the absurd hypothesis that somehow the religious instinct is no part of the workingman's nature, we are forced to think either that the food that is fitted to satisfy is not offered or that the partaking of it is hedged round with conditions which even the religious instinct revolts against. Think for a moment: on the simplest assumptions of the Christian religion can we for a moment admit that, where real Christianity in its completeness is offered to men, the masses will reject it and not even feel their loss?

Again, it is said that the Church is suffering partial paralysis due to her lack of whole-hearted sympathy with the modern intellect; that she desires light, yet distrusts the light-bringers—distrusts the only persons who have so loved the truth as to bear the toil and endure the pain of searching for it where alone it can be found. Suppose, once more, that we grant the premises for the sake of seeing what follows. Is it conceivable that ignorance is so strongly intrenched in the Church that the modern intellect could not dislodge it even with its mighty modern weapons? Why does not the intellectual world care enough for the Church to save her from her ignorance? Why is it so easy, whenever ecclesiastical ignorance withstands knowledge, for the men of learning to avoid the natural conflict? Why are intellectual men so much at home outside the Church, or in only nominal connection with it?

Questions like these open up many avenues for reflection. We might talk of methods of Church work; of the education of the clergy demanded by our times; of the spiritual ministries springing up outside the Church; of the very conception of the function of the Church in the world. But none of these can quite take the place of perhaps the most fundamental question of all—the constitution and modes of working of the human mind with which we have to deal. What are the basal needs of this nature, and what has the Christian religion to offer for their satisfaction? If any large factor in the community becomes cold toward existing modes of organized religion the question becomes pertinent whether the Church is as broad as human nature. This problem must be freshly canvassed in every age, lest methods and instituitions become obstacles rather than instruments of the spirit and the life.

If we view the problem psychologically we shall feel perfectly safe in assuming that any large and persistent excess of women in the Churches is chiefly due to a superior adaptation of Church life to the female nature. It is because the Church looks at things with feminine eyes, and calls chiefly into exercise the faculties in which women excel men. In fact, the explanation has been given in the whole analysis of religious phenomena contained in the present chapter and in Chapter III.

James Russell Lowell, speaking of the American

of the future, remarks that his religion will be more than

> "an ambulance
> To fetch life's wounded and malingerers in,
> Scorned by the strong." [1]

"Scorned by the strong"—that is the rebuke that stings. And it stings because of the measure of truth it conveys. The practical question that emerges, then, is whether masculine strength would not be drawn to us if we only put proportional stress upon the more rugged, active, intellectual, and social virtues—if we only held up the complete ideal for humanity with not even a fragment lacking.

If it is wise to learn from one's enemies, it is possible to believe that even Nietsche may not have been in absolute error when, in his burning accusation against Christianity, he charges, among other things, that it worships weakness where it should worship strength.[2] There is a lesson for us, furthermore, in the popular impression that there is a tendency to ultra-femininity in Sunday school instruction. The namby-pamby, goody-goody conception of goodness is simply an exaggeration, amounting to a caricature, of the gentler virtues in which women excel. Such an ideal will, of course, lose its influence over boys at least as soon as they approach manhood.

---

[1] " The Cathedral."
[2] See his *Antichrist*, in vol. xi of his Works, New York, 1896.

The temperamental interpretation of Christianity is likewise one probable reason for the aloofness from the Church of a strangely large proportion of the most high-minded, morally earnest, and intelligent men and women. These persons live correct lives and reverence God; if their names were on the roll of a church no one would question their piety. Some of them would find an obstacle to Church membership in the credal vows required in many of the Churches, but most of them would not. Indeed, it is probable that only a small proportion of them could allege any specific and adequate reason why they should not belong to some Church. The fact seems to be that Church life and ideals do not appeal to them. In much the same mood are many of our members who have the capacity, if it were only in active exercise, to be strong leaders and workers. Their attitude toward current forms of spiritual culture—such as are found in the prayer meeting, for example—is one of indifference, if it is not actually hostile. If it were possible to determine by a census what proportion of the moral and intellectual strength of the average community, and particularly of the city community, is actively employed in what is commonly called the spiritual work of the Church, what disheartening figures we should read! It is probably no exaggeration to say that the average man of culture and moral earnestness, though he may look upon the Church as a useful institution, and hence worthy of his financial support, nevertheless feels little personal need of its peculiar ministrations.

This attitude must be regarded as a grave mistake, and from many points of view. For surely we are not quite ready either to get along without churches or to admit that the Church as a whole has a specific mission to none but the less fortunate classes. Shall we, then, as spiritual self-complacency would prompt us to do, assume that the whole difficulty lies in the men whom the Church fails to draw to her heart? Shall we say that a merely temporary breeze of worldliness has carried them a little way from their moorings and that they will yet be brought back to the unchanged Church? To very many observers, who believe in the mission of the Church to all men, such views appear utterly fatuous. Instead of soothing ourselves by self-righteous assumption, should we not rather ask after more facts? Instead of accusing those whom we fail to draw, might we not well seek to understand the actual process of their minds, and thus discover whether the Church is offering spiritual refreshment and modes of spiritual activity actually adapted to the many-sided human personality? Perhaps it is not the depravity, but rather the spiritual hunger, of men that deters them.

So much for point of view. Now for the application of our own results. If our judgment as to

the one-sidedness of the traditional conception of
spirituality is just, then we ought to expect precisely such an alienation of strong men and women
from the Church as we actually discover. We
should expect to find a general lack of sympathy
which might attach itself to any one of many superficial faults in the Church but would not be explained by any or all of them. In a word, the known
results are natural consequences of a cause which
we have shown to exist. The difficulty is a mal-
adjustment of temperaments—nothing less general,
less constitutional, or less intangible than that. Not
but that many other sources of difficulty coexist
with this one; our claim is not to have laid bare the
sole cause, but only one real and profound one.
The remedy is easily defined, at least in its broader
aspects. It is the universalizing of Church life and
ideals through recognition of the fact that spiritual
qualities and needs run through the whole gamut
of human faculties. The spiritual conceit of the
melancholic temperament must be resisted. The
spiritual trivialities of the sanguine must be tran-
scended. The spirituality of the moral will and of
the truth-loving intellect must be not merely con-
ceded, but preached, insisted upon, gloried in. This
is the foundation upon which the rebuilding must
proceed.

The proposal thus to broaden the psychological
basis of Church life and ideals has immediate bear-

ing upon the most vital special questions of the day. A few of these questions may be mentioned, as, for instance, the essentially social and this-world nature of the kingdom of God and of salvation; the problem of institutional Churches; reform in revival methods; simplification of the conditions of Church membership; the struggle for greater flexibility in matters of creed; how to accept new light with regard to the Bible without first fighting against it and being beaten; the movement for increased co-operation and ultimate union of the Churches. This is not the place for discussing any of these weighty matters. But such discussion should certainly be grounded upon a sound judgment concerning the psychological soil out of which religion as well as other elements of civilization must grow.

The Fleeting and the Permanent in Christian Experience.

As a relief from these more or less disquieting suggestions let us go back once more for a parting glimpse of the Christian experience of which Churches are an outcome and an expression. In the *questionnaire* to which reference was made in the earlier chapters the following question was asked: "What is there in religion that seems to you permanent, that is, within your reach at any and all times? Do not give your theory of how it ought to be, but simply state what you yourself have found that you can absolutely rely upon." The number of answers received in response to this question was 52, 35 being from men and 17 from women. They may be classified as follows:

	Of 35 men.	Of 17 women.	Of total 52.
1. Divine help, strength, etc...................	14	11	25
2. Something connected with right and wrong, as truth of Christ's principle of self-sacrifice, Christ the center and source of life, meaning in life, sense of having done duty, peace from doing God's will, obligation recognized as God's will, peace to a troubled conscience, moral ideals, brotherhood of man, something to live for......................	10	1	11
3. Something connected with prayer and promises, as Bible promises sure, Christ and his word of truth, power of prayer, willingness to answer prayer....	4	0	4
4. Social feelings, as friendship, love, or companionship of God or of Christ, sympathy, comfort, trust, sense of God's presence......................	13	14	27
5. Something connected with forgiveness, as pardoning power, assurance of acceptance...................	3	0	3
6. Miscellaneous, as rest, peace, joy, no fear, refuge from disappointments, omniscience of God, assurance of eternal life...........................	4	3	7

There are several things about this table that might well attract attention. In the first place, it illustrates in a new way the already known fact that men vary more than women. For, while nearly all the answers from women can be bunched in two classes, the answers from the men run through a larger scale and are less bunched at any point. Again, as indicated in a previous section, while the women far exceed the men in mentioning feelings of social relationship to God and help from God, the men exceed the women even more strikingly in designating matters connected with right and wrong, with prayer and forgiveness.

But perhaps the most significant point of all, at

least for our present purpose, is the diversity of gifts in the unity of the Spirit—the varying accents of the Holy Ghost. Approximately half of the writers did not mention divine aid as a permanent fact in their experience. Doubtless it is a permanent fact, but this particular aspect of the Christian's privilege certainly appeals to some devout minds far less than it does to others. Similarly, nearly half the writers fail to mention social feeling toward God or Christ as permanent. Now, in all probability some feeling like that of communion is approximately, if not absolutely, universal and permanent; yet it occupies the attention and thought of some much more than of others. It is not the most powerful lever.

An inspection of the table just given will show that the first three groups are relatively homogeneous, while the remaining groups form a second homogeneous set differing from the former. Reclassifying upon this new basis, we secure another angle from which to view the facts:

	Of 35 men.	Of 17 women.	Of total 52.
Help, invigoration of the will, something connected with duty	28	12	40
Various kinds of satisfactory feeling	20	17	37

This represents, not the number of times certain qualities come to expression, but the number of persons giving answers of each kind. The most that need be claimed for this result is that it is significant of a trend. It is a straw which shows the direction of the wind. But the evidence, as far as it goes, tends to show that the strength of Christianity lies as much in its appeal to the moral will as in its appeal to feeling. This is true of the general average. But in the case of the men the preponderance of the moral will becomes very marked. If the answers that mentioned pardon, which came exclusively from men, were to be classified with the group called "something connected with right and wrong," the exhibit would be still more nearly conclusive. If, now, the fact be noted that these answers were obtained almost exclusively from persons brought up under the influence of a Church that cultivates religious emotions more than any other of the large denominations of Christians; and if, furthermore, the fact be noted that the writers were still within hailing distance of the sentimental age of life, the results gain enhanced significance. What they suggest to us is that however much we cultivate religious feelings we cannot touch the whole of human nature—of the religious nature—until we learn that states of the will as well as of the sensibility are included in religious experience. In particular, with men it is in the sphere of the moral will that religion makes its most abiding impression.

It does not belong to the scope of this discussion to show in detail how the Christian religion appeals to the will, invigorates it, prescribes its ideals, and even through it reacts upon both the intellectual and the emotional faculties. Nor can we here inquire what has been universal and what merely occasional in the religious experience of the Church as a whole through all the Christian centuries. But it is safe to say that a study of the history of Christianity with a view to answering this question would prove to be a most illuminating and invigorating exercise. As a starting point for such a study, we may glance, in conclusion, at

The Mind of the Master.

What shall we say of Jesus's mental organization, and of his attitude toward life, looked at from a purely psychological point of view? The difficulties in the quest for such knowledge are very large; for, not only were there no modern eyes to observe Jesus, and no modern motives for observing him, but also the literary medium through which we get our only glimpses of him is itself more or less of a psychological problem. Perhaps nothing, moreover, is more difficult than to free ourselves from the peculiar atmospheric perspective with which history, and particularly the Roman Church, has enveloped everything connected with the life of Christ. The Church has represented him as the prince of ascetics, and art in large degree has adopted the ecclesiastical conception. This conception has attained a most instructive concrete representation in the Passion Play at Oberammergau. The full resources of the highest modern dramatic art are here poured out to make vivid and impressive the figure of the Man of Sorrows. It is, in fact, difficult to imagine how the Roman conception could have a more perfect setting forth to eye and ear. The design is unquestionably artistic, the execution adequate to the design. Undoubtedly art values and religious values are there. But what is the design thus wrought into forms of sense? It is simply pathos, or suffering innocence personified. I speak of the play as it was presented the last time (1890). The figure of Jesus as portrayed by Josef Mayer was that of a purely passive sufferer. At times the sufferer seemed to be dazed, benumbed, by the continuous pain; again he seemed to make a virtue of suffering, as though, if the expression may be allowed, he was a supreme specialist in that art. The fullness of manhood which the theory of Christ's person demands was not discernible.

Nietsche, endeavoring to analyze the person of Christ from the standpoint of modern psychology and neurology, proclaimed that Jesus was a degenerate and a neurotic.[1] But I think it can be shown that Nietsche got his general notion of the facts less from the first sources than from the eccle-

---

[1] *Antichrist*, in vol. xi of his Works, 1896.

siastical tradition. It is not strange, to be sure, that he who, of all men, was most a man of sorrows should, in a sorrowful world like ours, be commonly portrayed as a sufferer. But it may be doubted whether either art or religious instruction has at all adequately set forth the victorious element in his whole character and career. We hardly grasp the meaning of the suffering itself until we perceive that it expressed not only exquisite sensibility, not only the pathos of utter injustice, but also marvelous resoluteness and persistence of will—nay, the carrying out of a plan through and by means of this very suffering. The pains he had to bear, that is, do not stand for a passive but rather an active personality. To refer to a single illustration of this point, not a parallel case, we may ask whether it would not work historical injustice if, in thinking and speaking of John Brown, we habitually fixed attention upon the pains he had to endure as a consequence or even as part of his plan instead of upon the central inspiration of his life. Similarly, to think of Jesus as incarnate pathos more than as incarnate heroism is a perversion of fact.

This implies that his strength of will was not the same as that of the ascetics. The difference in this respect between him and, say, Peter the Hermit is that between a healthy will, able to stand erect amid all the jostling interests and all the buffetings of life, and one that has the appearance of strength only because it has been concentrated by an unhealthy process of self-inversion.

It is time to see and proclaim that Jesus was not a sentimental, or melancholic, or introspective mind. We are told that he is not known to have smiled but is known to have wept; and yet he entered most fully into the gayety of the marriage feast, and accepted the simple pleasures of life so whole-heartedly that he was accused of being a glutton and a winebibber. If we would but look to see we should find an active and penetrating and objective intellect shining through his teachings. We should also find a robust as well as controlled will, not merely when he cleansed the temple, but in many a vicissitude in which weak men would have quailed.[1]

In his teachings, too, he explicitly guarded against the narrowing down of religion to temperamental qualities. The sentimentality of Mary was not preferred above the practical activity of Martha, but only Mary's choice of that which brings unity and repose of spirit into the multitudinous duties of life. As soon as Zacchæus decided upon a course of righteous living Jesus announced that salvation had come to him. Jesus's answer to the young man who wanted to know how to attain eternal life, his declaration of the principle of the final judgment, and his summary of duty in the two great commandments, all are unequivocal in placing the cen-

[1] Thomas Hughes, *The Manliness of Christ.*

ter of gravity of spiritual life in the attitude of the will.

In Jesus and the religion which he teaches, then, spirituality is complete because all-sided. It rests upon nothing incidental to environment or peculiar to any temperament. What he commands and commends is realizable by all.

APPENDIX A

Questionnaire on Religious Experience

THE sole purpose of the following questions is to discover the actual processes of the mind in its religious experiences. It is believed that definite scientific knowledge of these processes may be made of no small assistance in religious work, training, and self-culture. Your answers will be treated as confidential if you so desire. If there is any marked fact in your religious life which the questions do not bring out, please describe it. Kindly write your answers in ink, on only one side of each sheet, and leave a margin of one inch at top of each sheet.

1. Sex.
2. Name.
3. Age.
4. What blood predominates in your veins (for example, English, Scotch, Irish, German, Norwegian, etc.)?
5. What Church are you a member of?
6. Were you brought up under the influence of this Church?
7. At what age did you join?
8. State your age at each period of marked religious awakening in your life. By religious awakening is meant a deep impression that

261

you ought to be religious, that you ought to
attain a higher level of religious life, etc.

9. Indicate in a word what each of these periods
of awakening led to, as, for example, conversion, sanctification, joining the Church
or being confirmed, restoration after falling,
reconsecration after a period of coldness,
etc. If nothing came of it, say so.

10. Describe your experiences in each of these periods, taking the periods one by one.

For example, did you experience sorrow for
sin, and if so, was it for specific sins that you
knew you had committed? Was it for a
bad temper, or other bad qualities of heart
or character? Or was it for something else?

Were you afraid of anything, as the wrath of
God, hell, etc.?

State any doubts that troubled you.

What was your most intense desire at the time?

What did you think you ought to be that you
were not already?

What did you do about it?

What did you hope or expect would be the result? State as exactly as you can what you
had faith for (removal of the sense of guilt?
joy? peace? victory over a certain temptation or fault? help in doing some hard duty?
love for your enemies? sense of God's presence or love?).

How did it come out? How were you different
in feeling, etc., from what you were before?
Make your answer very specific.

Did you hear any voices? See any visions?
Have any remarkable dream? Experience
any physical manifestations?

Did you experience the witness of the Spirit or
assurance?

Did any of these phenomena change very soon?
If so, what ones, and how soon did each
change?

Were you entirely satisfied with your new experience? If not, what was lacking?

What part did God seem to have in this entire
series of events? What made you think so?
The question is not what you now believe,
but what you *then* felt and thought about it.

Add any other facts that will help to make clear
just what went on in your own mind at these
times.

11. What influenced you in each of these cases
(for example, the Bible, a sermon, the personal solicitude of some one else, seeing
others start, the death of a friend, or the
general trend of things at the time)?

If you were influenced by revival meetings, describe the method of conducting the meetings, and what there was about them that
particularly moved you.

If you prayed, what did you pray for, and how did the answers come?

Did the example, experiences, or conversation of others move you? If so, tell what they did or said, and how it affected you.

If you were affected by music, tell what the music was and what effect it had upon you.

If you made a decision of any sort, what was it, and how did you come to make it?

Were other persons passing through the same experiences and making the same decisions as yourself? How many others?

Was any person whom you very much admired or very much disliked in any way connected with these events? If so, what was it you admired or disliked in him, and what did he have to do with your experiences at the time?

What delayed, hindered, rendered painful, or altogether prevented the advance in religious life that you felt you ought to make?

Add any other facts that will help to make clear what influences were playing upon you at the time.

12. Describe your religious environment in childhood.

For example, what members of your family were religious, and what ones were not?

Did you know the history of your parents' re-

ligious experience? If so, give a brief outline of it.

What did they teach you about religion? Especially about what one does and experiences
in conversion?

If conversions, etc., took place among members
of the family, give a brief outline of the circumstances, and tell how you were affected
thereby.

Was there family prayer? Were definite answers to prayer expected, and were they received? If so, give an example or two.

Were you aware that your parents, pastor, or
Sunday school teacher regarded you as a
sinner?

Was anybody very anxious about your conversion? Did you know it at the time?

What was looked upon by yourself and the persons about you as evidence that one was
converted?

How did you come to realize that you were a
rebel against God?

In short, name anything in your childhood environment that tended to affect your religious development.

13. What were your religious habits in childhood?

Were you in the habit of praying? Describe
any answers to your prayers.

Were you in the habit of performing any other

private religious exercises? If so, name
them.

Did you ever seem to see God, or to hear his
voice? Or did he seem to come to you in
any other way? Describe the experience.

Were you habitually wicked? If so, did you
realize it at the time, and what were then
your thoughts about God, etc.? If you are
willing to do so, state the general direction
your wickedness took.

If not habitually wicked, did you have a besetting sin into which you occasionally fell?
If you are willing to do so, indicate its general nature. How did you feel about this
sin, and about your relation to God?

When you resisted a temptation or did a hard
duty, did you seem to have help from God?
What made you think that he helped you?

Were you conscious of his approval when you
did right, and of his disapproval when you
did wrong? How did this differ from the
approval and disapproval of conscience? In
your answer to this question distinguish
carefully between what you then felt and
what you now think about it.

Did you perform any public religious duties,
such as going to church, partaking the communion, speaking in meeting? Tell what
services you were accustomed to attend, the

age at which you began to attend each, and
the age at which you ceased to attend.

Which service impressed you most, and *how*
did it impress you?

Were any marked religious phenomena, such as
conversions, sanctifications, etc., taking
place about you? Did you witness any?
Hear testimonies of any? Give brief description of the ones that most impressed
you.

If your notions of religious experience subsequently underwent any transformation, tell
what the change was and how it came about.

14. Have you had ups and downs in your religious
experience?

If so, what is it that has been irregular (for example, joy, peace, trust and worry, certainty
and doubt of your acceptance, fervor and
coldness in prayer, delight in duty)?

How frequent have these changes been?

Name any causes that you have been able to
discover (for example, good and ill health,
overwork, influence of worldly or spiritual
associates, willful sin, deliberate determination to do a duty, new theories about religion, new insight into the Bible, etc.). Have
the "ups" of a particular kind generally occurred in a particular season of the year, and
have the corresponding "downs" generally

occurred in a particular season? What seasons? Have persons about you exhibited the same variations?

Look over the marked changes in your circumstances in life—such as occupation, place of residence, social surroundings or associates, pastor, teachers, lines of reading or study—and tell whether changes in your religious life have been coincident with these other changes. State the direction of the change in each case.

How does your present religious feeling differ from that of the period just following your conversion?

If you have never been converted, state how your feelings with respect to God have changed since childhood. Do you find any difference in the approvals and disapprovals of conscience?

If you have been entirely sanctified, describe the difference between your habitual feelings at present and those that were habitual before.

What is there in religion that seems to you permanent, that is within your reach at any and all times? Do not give your theory of how it ought to be, but simply state what you yourself have found that you can absolutely rely upon.

15. At what periods in your life has your health

been at its best? When has it not been good? Include in your answer all instances of prolonged nervous exhaustion, excessive nervousness, debility, etc. If you are willing to do so, name the defect of health with each period. If you are unwilling to state the particular difficulty, designate the fact simply as "fit of sickness," "not in my usual health," "not strong," etc.

What was the state of your health at each of the periods mentioned in questions?

16. What kind of work, play, books, studies, natural scenery, music, poems, acquaintances, social gatherings, conversation, and religious exercises do you like best, and which do you most dislike?

If you were obliged to spend a whole day alone, felt at perfect liberty to follow your inclinations, and had the means to do so, what would you do?

What sort of things or persons annoy you most?

Do you laugh and cry easily? Do you make friends easily? Do your friendships last?

Do you get angry or indignant easily? Do you get over anger or indignation quickly? When you get angry, which of the following is most likely to happen: long brooding over the wound? weeping? loud words? an

18   269

immediate effort to "get even," or to correct the wrong? deliberate and cold-blooded planning to do so?

Are you accustomed to have deep fears, long-ings, the blues, or other moods that last a long time? If you are willing to do so, give examples.

Is it hard for you to abandon a task which you have undertaken but not completed? Give examples. Does any ambition or ideal stir you to the depths? How long has it done so?

Are you very bashful? Do you suffer from any other form of sensitiveness?

Do you think a great deal about your future?

Are you accustomed to examine yourself, weigh your motives, estimate your spiritual health?

Are you prompt or hesitating in your decisions, especially in small matters? Have you al-ways been so? If you are hesitating, tell how you finally make the move.

Do you enjoy active physical exercise?

Do you ever get worn out with excitement? If so, describe or name a few occasions on which this has happened.

Have you ever had a vision of an absent or dead friend? Ever heard the voice of such a friend? Ever seen or heard anything that could not be accounted for as an ordinary act of perception? Particularly, have you ever heard voices, either coming to you from outside, or seeming to come from within? If you have had any of these experiences (which are common), relate the circumstances. Be particular to say how often you have had each kind of manifestation.

APPENDIX B

Plan for the Observation of Temperament

1. Name.
2. Age.
3. Sex.
4. Nationality.
5. Color of hair.
6. Of eyes.
7. Complexion.
8. Stout or thin.
9. General health.
10. Are the eyes active and restless? Are they intense and penetrating? Are they dull and expressionless?
11. Do face and manner indicate that he is wide-awake to his surroundings, or does he seem, rather, to be chiefly occupied with his own thoughts? Does he have an absent-minded air, or a far-away and dreamy look?
12. Is the facial expression placid? Are the muscles of the face drawn as if through mental intensity? Does he draw down his eyebrows? Are there strongly marked perpendicular furrows between the eyes? Is he very deliberate?
13. Is the voice shrill and high-keyed? Does he

speak very rapidly, or very slowly? Does he
speak before he thinks?

14. Do his muscles seem to be habitually relaxed?
If not, do they seem to be habitually con-
tracted? Are his motions quick and wiry,
or more moderate, free, and pendulum-like?
Are they very slow?

15. Which is more characteristic of him: receiving
impressions from his surroundings, or active
effort to control or change his surroundings?

16. Is he easily persuaded? If not, is it because of
(a) a habit of deliberation, (b) contrari-
ness, or (c) mere inertia?

17. Is he a warm and intense or cold and passion-
less soul? Does he get angry or indignant
easily? Does he get over it quickly? When
he is angry or indignant, which of the following are characteristic of him? (a) Ready
feeling without action; (b) Intense feeling
with immediate action, speech included; (c)
Feeling too feeble to produce very positive
action; (d) Tendency to brood over his indignation, but not to act; (e) Tendency to
plan deliberate revenge or the improvement
of conditions, and action to that end in cool
blood; (f) Fixed and unchangeable aversion.

18. Does he change easily from one activity to another (for example, is he persistent in what
he undertakes, loyal to his friends, obstinate,

THE SPIRITUAL LIFE

"pig-headed," fickle, etc.) ? Does he make acquaintances easily? If he is fickle, does he change about from mere impulse, or from calculation? If he is constant, is it from principle, or is it merely because he tends to keep going in any direction after he has once started? Has he a strong sense of consistency?

19. Has he a cheerful disposition? Does he get the blues? If so, is the mood intense, and how long does it generally last? What other pronounced moods does he have, and how long do they last? Is he given to criticising? If so, does he take it out in merely finding fault, or does he brood over what he criticises, or does he work for improvement? If he works for improvement, are his efforts impetuous and spasmodic, or steady and persistent?

20. Which of the following characterize his intellect? (*a*) Quickness; (*b*) Accuracy; (*c*) Slowness; (*d*) Inaccuracy; (*e*) Clearness of insight; (*f*) Breadth of information; (*g*) System; (*h*) Lack of system; (*i*) Receptivity, or ability to understand; (*j*) Fondness for finding out things for himself, and not resting in what he is told.

21. Is he oversensitive in the way of bashfulness; of overconscientiousness; of self-deprecia-

tion? Is he given to introspection? Is he troubled by doubts and fears? Is he hard to get acquainted with?

22. Is he self-assertive? If so, what direction does the self-assertiveness take (for example, does he monopolize conversation; break in when others are speaking; stoutly contradict opinions that differ from his own; become quarrelsome when he cannot convince; make undue effort to control his associates)? What is the effect of his not having his own way? Does it depress his feelings, or rouse him to more intense antagonism or self-assertion?

23. Which of the following characterize his religious life? (*a*) Rapid rise and fall of feeling, or change from one feeling to another. Does he have to be revived every winter? Is his conduct unsteady? Or his religious activities? (*b*) Prevalence of happy mood. Does it ever become ecstatic? (*c*) Prevalence of unhappy mood, such as anxiety, sorrow for sins of himself or of the Church, censoriousness, discouragement, etc. (*d*) The revival spirit, always wanting to have something going on, fondness for excitement. Indicate whether this issues in persistent work, or spasmodic effort, or no work at all. (*e*) Wide sympathy with suffering humanity.

(*f*) Philanthropic activities. Are they steady or spasmodic? (*g*) Meditation on the goodness of God, the awfulness of sin, the sufferings of Christ, the blessings of grace, etc. (*h*) Intellectual attitude toward religion. Chief emphasis upon truth. Is he conservative; radical; bigoted and intolerant?

24. Name his most prominent characteristic, all things considered. Is this the general opinion of him? Name any apparent contradiction in his nature, that is, union of opposite qualities.

276

INDEX

277

Index

279